SOUTHWESTERN WEAVING

This catalog presents the southwestern textile collection of the Maxwell Museum of Anthropology at the University of New Mexico. It is published as a joint venture of the Maxwell Museum and the UNM Press.

SOUTHWESTERN WEAVING

Marian E. Rodee

UNIVERSITY OF NEW MEXICO PRESS Albuquerque

CONTENTS

This book was made possible by a grant from the National Endowment for the Arts, No. R 50-20127, Amendment 3-76.

ACKNOWLEDGMENTS

The Museum would like to express its appreciation to all the people who have donated textiles to its collection. Special thanks go to Mr. Gilbert Maxwell whose personal collection forms the nucleus of ours and also to Mr. Edwin Kennedy whose interest in sandpainting weaving has given us a superlative selection of these textiles.

This catalog, made possible by a grant from the National Endowment for the Arts, was written to assist museum professionals and students of weaving in their research. The photographs, technical information, and documentation (when present) of the weaving will indicate our resources for specialists. It is our hope that it will also be of interest to non-specialized collectors and the general reader.

I would also like to extend my personal thanks to several people, especially Joe Ben Wheat of the University of Colorado who identified and dated several of our textiles. Credit also goes to Caroline Olin of Santa Fe for locating the sources for many of our sandpainting design rugs. Thanks are due to the other staff members of the Museum, especially Director J. J. Brody, for his encouragement, editorial assistance, and expeditious organization of the entire project. Last of all, my sincere thanks to Sally Black for her technical assistance in preparing the manuscript.

The following definitions are used to describe each textile in the catalog.

DATE   Known dates of manufacture and of collection are specified as such. Most other dates are educated guesses based on style and materials.

ACCESSION NUMBER   The three-part number on the second line of each catalog entry. Each item is identified within the Museum by this number.

SIZE   Length always precedes width. Dimensions are expressed in centimeters and are taken to the nearest half-centimeter. The width is always measured across the warps regardless of the pattern.

COUNT   The fineness of textiles is expressed by the number of warps and wefts per inch. Where there is a significant difference in fineness from one yarn to another, this is noted.

EDGE FINISH   On continuous warp Navajo and Pueblo weaving only the weft selvage cords are described. On Spanish-American textiles the cut warp ends are also noted.   KNOTTED CHAIN   is used to describe a variation of the simple knotting of warps common in finishing Spanish-American textiles. Each one of a pair of warps is knotted with one warp of a neighboring pair to give a chain-like effect.

WEAVE   Unless otherwise stated all textiles in the Navajo and Pueblo sections are in the tapestry technique.   PLAIN   Weft threads pass alternately over and under successive warps.   BALANCED OR 50/50 PLAIN WEAVE   Warp and weft elements are equally spaced and similar in size.   WARP-FACED   Plain weave with the warps concealing the wefts because they are more closely spaced and numerous than the wefts.   WEFT-FACED   Plain weave in which the wefts conceal the warps.

TAPESTRY   Weft-faced plain weave with the introduction of mosaic-like colored areas built up by weaving the wefts back and forth within each individual area.   TWILL   A single weft passed over and under two or more warps, with each row staggered.   WARP FLOAT   Patterns are introduced by passing (or floating) warps over weft elements.   WRAPPED BROCADE   Patterns are made by floating yarn across the surface of loosely woven plain weave fabric and wrapping it around one or two warps, producing thick ridges in the textile.

TYPE OF YARN   HANDSPUN   Spun with a Navajo or Pueblo spindle or a Spanish-American spinning wheel.   COMMERCIAL   Factory made yarn processed by machine. Generally 3- or 4-ply. Weavers sometimes separate 4-ply yarn into 2-ply elements. Terms such as "Saxony" and "Germantown" are avoided in the descriptions. What was once termed Saxony is described here as 3-ply vegetal dyed commercial yarn, and Germantown as 3-ply or 4-ply aniline dyed commercial yarn. RAVELED Yarn made by separating the individual threads of a piece of commercially manufactured cloth and respinning. STRING Commercially manufactured cotton twine or string.

SPIN The direction in which a fiber is spun. It is called S or Z according to whether it was twisted in a right- or left-handed direction.

PLY The twisting together of two or more strands of yarn.

TWIST The direction in which the yarn goes (S or Z) when it is plied. It is always the opposite direction from the spin.

DYES NATURAL The color of the wool as it comes from the sheep (after cleaning). NATURAL+ Usually a natural brown or black fleece with vegetal coloring added. Aniline used to enhance the color is specified. CARDED Two colors blended or carded together to produce a third. For example, gray made by blending black and white wool, or pink by mixing red and white. VEGETAL The term used here is synonymous with the words native or natural, and refers to dyes made from plant and animal products. Although it is not completely accurate, since animal dyes are included, it is customary usage. When the specific organic material is known this is noted. COCHINEAL A dye ranging in color from scarlet to rose/red, orange, or purple obtained from crushing a small parasitic beetle which lives on cactus. INDIGO A vegetal dye grown commercially in Guatemala and the Carolinas during the nineteenth century. It is usually dark to pale blue in color but can be mixed with native yellow, usually from the rabbit brush, to produce a bright green. ANILINE Commercially manufactured dyes obtained from coaltar derivatives. First manufactured in Europe in 1856.

1
NAVAJO TEXTILES

The Nineteenth Century

The Classic Period (1800–80)

It is not known exactly when the Navajos arrived in the Southwest or when they learned to weave. They were weaving by the late eighteenth century and probably even earlier, but examples that predate 1800 are rare. Most early Navajo textiles were wearing blankets and had a reputation for quality and watertightness.

The earliest example of Navajo weaving in the Museum's collection is one of several recovered from Massacre Cave, Canyon de Chelly, Arizona. In the winter of 1804–05 a group of Navajos, including women and children, were discovered hiding in a cave and killed by a party of Spanish soldiers on a reprisal mission. The site was undisturbed until 1914 when it came to the attention of Sam Day, a local trader. Day recovered a number of textiles and sold them to collectors and museums so that examples from Massacre Cave are now scattered throughout the country. A fragment cut from our piece (no. 1), a brown and white striped wool blanket, is in the collection of the Laboratory of Anthropology, Museum of New Mexico, Santa Fe.

The Museum has no Navajo textiles made between 1800 and about 1850, the early part of the so-called classic weaving period. *Bayeta*, the Spanish name for a commercially manufactured English baize or flannel cloth, was brought into the Southwest via two routes: from England to Spain, Mexico City, and points north, or after 1823 over the Santa Fe Trail from St. Louis. The Navajos unraveled it from the original bolt of cloth, respun, and rewove it into blankets. The most popular color used by the Navajo was cochineal dyed red. Although cochineal was available to weavers in the Saltillo district of northern Mexico (see the third chapter of this catalog), it was almost never used on handspun wool by the Navajo and was used very infrequently by the Spanish weavers of the Rio Grande Valley. Cochineal dye did not reach New Mexico in any quantity, so that the Navajo were forced to unravel red dyed cloth to obtain this color for their own weaving. Another alien product of the classic period was machine-spun Saxony yarn made from the silky fleece of Saxony sheep dyed with organic materials such as cochineal and indigo.

The dominant colors of classic weaving are red, white, blue, and black and the most prevalent design elements are stripes and terraced diamonds. There is a clearly defined evolution from simple groups of stripes—as in the Massacre Cave blanket—to the alternating stripes, diamonds, and zigzags of the 1860s and 1870s. However, plain stripes continued to be popular until about 1900 and striped (or banded) textiles are occasionally made today.

1

Blanket
63.34.69

Date: before 1804
Gift of Mr. and Mrs. Gilbert Maxwell
(large section) and Mr. R. Plummer
(small section)

Two fragments from Massacre Cave, Canyon de Chelly.
See Maxwell 1963:10, fig. 1, and Kahlenberg and Berlant 1972:21.

Size: 119 cm. x 134.5 cm.
Count: 4 warps, 12 wefts.
Selvage: over last warp, no cord.

	Fiber	Type of Yarn	Spin	Twist	Ply	Color	Dye
Warp	Wool	Handspun	Z		1	Brown	Natural
	Wool	Handspun	Z		1	Beige	Natural
Weft	Wool	Handspun	Z		1	Dark brown	Natural
	Wool	Handspun	Z		1	Beige	Natural
	Wool	Handspun	Z		1	Med. brown	Natural

2

Blanket
65.47.2

Date: ca. 1850–1900
Gift of Dr. W. W. Hill

Bought in Chinle in 1934.

Size: 176.5 cm. x 130 cm.
Count: 7 warps, 16 wefts.
Selvage: two cords; 2-ply white natural handspun.

	Fiber	Type of Yarn	Spin	Twist	Ply	Color	Dye
Warp	Wool	Handspun	Z		1	White	Natural
Weft	Wool	Handspun	Z		1	White	Natural
	Wool	Handspun	Z		1	Dark brown	Natural
	Wool	Handspun	Z		1	Med. brown	Natural
	Wool	Handspun	Z		1	Beige	Carded

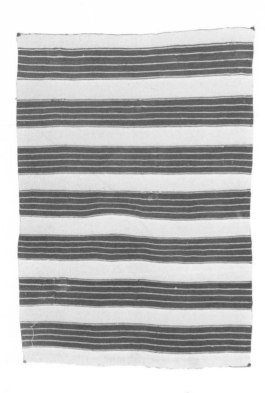

3

Blanket
63.34.104

Date: 1850–1900
Gift of Mr. and Mrs. Gilbert Maxwell

Purchased from Fred Harvey Co. 1955.

Size: 172 cm. x 127 cm.
Count: 6 warps, 24 wefts.
Selvage: two cords; 2-ply light and dark blue indigo dyed
   handspun.

	Fiber	Type of Yarn	Spin	Twist	Ply	Color	Dye
Warp	Wool	Handspun	Z		1	Brown	Natural
Weft	Wool	Handspun	Z		1	Brown	Natural+
	Wool	Handspun	Z	1	1	Blue	Indigo
	Wool	Handspun	Z		1	White	Natural

4

Blanket/Rug
65.46.1

Date: 1870–80
Gift of Mrs. W. H. Loerpabel

Size: 177 cm. x 137 cm.
Count: 6 warps, 18 wefts.
Selvage: two cords; 2-ply white handspun.

	Fiber	Type of Yarn	Spin	Twist	Ply	Color	Dye
Warp	Wool	Handspun	Z		1	Brown	Natural
Weft	Wool	Handspun	Z		1	White	Natural
	Wool	Handspun	Z		1	Dark brown	Natural+
	Wool	Handspun	Z		1	Blue	Indigo
	Wool	Handspun	Z		1	Purple	Cochineal & white carded

5

Blanket
63.34.139

Date: 1870–80
Gift of Mr. and Mrs. Gilbert Maxwell

Formerly in the Jim Seligman Collection.

Size: 184 cm. x 114 cm.
Count: 8 warps, 34 wefts.
Selvage: completely replaced.

	Fiber	Type of Yarn	Spin	Twist	Ply	Color	Dye
Warp	Wool	Handspun	Z		1	White	Natural
Weft	Wool	Handspun	Z		1	White	Natural
	Wool	Handspun	Z		1	Blue	Indigo
	Wool	Handspun	Z		1	Brown	Natural+

6

Blanket
63.34.123

Date: ca. 1860
Gift of Mr. and Mrs. Gilbert Maxwell

Formerly in the Earl Morris Collection.

Size: 176 cm. x 113.5 cm.
Count: 10 warps, 56 wefts (handspun) and 10 warps, 60 wefts
      (raveled).
Selvage: completely replaced.

	Fiber	Type of Yarn	Spin	Twist	Ply	Color	Dye
Warp	Wool	Handspun	Z		1	White	Natural
	Wool	Handspun	Z		1	Brown	Natural
Weft	Wool	Handspun	Z		1	Brown	Natural+
	Wool	Handspun	Z		1	White	Natural
	Wool	Handspun	Z		1	Blue	Indigo
	Wool	Raveled	Z	S	2	Red	Cochineal
	Wool	Raveled	Z	S	3	Red	Cochineal

7

Blanket
64.60.24

Date: 1860–75
Gift of Miss Erna Fergusson

Size: 144 cm. x 96 cm.
Count: 13 warps, 44 wefts.
Selvage: completely missing.

	Fiber	Type of Yarn	Spin	Twist	Ply	Color	Dye
Warp	Wool	Handspun	Z		1	White	Natural
Weft	Wool	Handspun	Z		1	White	Natural
	Wool	Handspun	Z		1	Dark blue	Indigo
	Wool	Handspun	Z		1	Med. blue	Indigo
	Wool	Raveled	Z	S	2	Red	Cochineal
	Wool	Raveled	Z	S	3	Red	Cochineal
	Wool	Handspun	Z		1	Green	Indigo & yellow

See plate section.

8

Blanket
63.34.122

Date: 1860–70
Gift of Mr. and Mrs. Gilbert Maxwell

Size: 151 cm. x 90 cm.
Count: 12 warps, 72 wefts.
Selvage: two cords; one 3-ply medium blue indigo dyed and one 3-ply natural brown.

	Fiber	Type of Yarn	Spin	Twist	Ply	Color	Dye
Warp	Wool	Handspun	Z		1	White	Natural
Weft	Wool	Handspun	Z		1	White	Natural
	Wool	Handspun	Z		1	Brown	Natural+
	Wool	Handspun	Z		1	Med. blue	Indigo
	Wool	Handspun	Z		1	Yellow	Vegetal
	Wool	Commercial	Z	S	3	Red	Cochineal
	Wool	Commercial	Z	S	3	Pink	Cochineal
	Wool	Raveled	S	Z	3	Red	Cochineal
	Wool	Raveled	Z	S	2	Red	Cochineal

9

Saddle Blanket
64.60.23

Date: 1860–70
Gift of Miss Erna Fergusson

Size: 66.5 cm. x 75.5 cm.
Count: 14 warps, 64 wefts.
Selvage: two cords; 2-ply light indigo dyed handspun.

	Fiber	Type of Yarn	Spin	Twist	Ply	Color	Dye
Warp	Wool	Handspun	Z		1	Brown	Natural
Weft	Wool	Handspun	Z		1	White	Natural
	Wool	Handspun	Z		1	Blue	Indigo
	Wool	Raveled	Z	S	3	Red	Cochineal

10

Double Saddle Blanket
63.34.124

Date: 1860–70
Gift of Mr. and Mrs. Gilbert Maxwell

Size: 135 cm. x 82.5 cm.
Count: 11 warps, 46 wefts.
Selvage: two cords; one 3-ply salmon pink vegetal dyed commercial yarn, 3-ply light yellow vegetal dyed commercial yarn. There is a break in the selvages 41 cm. from one end with small tassels as if for tying.

	Fiber	Type of Yarn	Spin	Twist	Ply	Color	Dye
Warp	Wool	Handspun	Z		1	White	Natural
Weft	Wool	Handspun	Z		1	White	Natural
	Wool	Handspun	Z		1	Blue	Indigo
	Wool	Commercial	Z	S	3	Red	Cochineal
	Wool	Handspun	Z		1	Pink	Cochineal
	Wool	Commercial	Z	S	3	Salmon pink	Cochineal

11

Blanket
63.34.119

Date: 1860–70
Gift of Mr. and Mrs. Gilbert Maxwell

Formerly in the Clay Lockett Collection.
See Maxwell 1963:41, fig. 34.

Size: 119.5 cm. x 87.5 cm.
Count: 13 warps, 50 wefts.
Selvage: two cords; 3-ply green (indigo plus yellow) handspun
and 3-ply indigo dyed handspun.

	Fiber	Type of Yarn	Spin	Twist	Ply	Color	Dye
Warp	Wool	Handspun	Z		1	White	Natural
Weft	Wool	Handspun	Z		1	White	Natural
	Wool	Handspun	Z		1	Blue	Indigo
	Wool	Raveled	Z		1	Green/ Yellow	Vegetal
	Wool	Raveled	Z	S	2	Green/ Yellow	Vegetal
	Wool	Raveled	Z	S	2	Red	Cochineal
	Wool	Commercial	S	Z	3	Red	Cochineal

See plate section.

12

Blanket
63.34.142

Date: 1870–80
Gift of Mr. and Mrs. Gilbert Maxwell

Collected by Stanley Stokes in 1880. Formerly in Frederick H.
Douglas Collection.
See Maxwell 1963:42, fig. 36.

Size: 286.5 cm. x 132 cm.
Count: 11 warps, 46 wefts.
Selvage: two cords; 3-ply cochineal dyed red commercial yarn.

	Fiber	Type of Yarn	Spin	Twist	Ply	Color	Dye
Warp	Wool	Handspun	Z		1	White	Natural
	Wool	Handspun	Z		1	Brown	Natural
Weft	Wool	Handspun	Z		1	Pink	Carded
	Wool	Handspun	Z		1	Blue	Indigo
	Wool	Handspun	Z		1	White	Natural
	Wool	Commercial	Z	S	3	Red	Cochineal
	Wool	Commercial	Z	S	3	Yellow	Vegetal
	Wool	Commercial	S	Z	3	Red	Cochineal

Note: The last yarn appears in a small band near edge. The yellow was once
a bright chartreuse.

13

Blanket
63.34.120

Date: 1870–80
Gift of Mr. and Mrs. Gilbert Maxwell

Formerly in Alfred Barton Collection.
See Maxwell 1963:42, fig. 35.

Size: 190.5 cm. x 34.5 cm.
Count: 12 warps, 48 wefts.
Selvage: two cords; 3-ply indigo dyed handspun.

See plate section.

	Fiber	*Type of Yarn*	*Spin*	*Twist*	*Ply*	*Color*	*Dye*
Warp	Cotton	String				White	Natural
	Wool	Handspun	Z		1	Brown	Natural
Weft	Wool	Handspun	Z		1	White	Natural
	Wool	Handspun	Z		1	Blue	Indigo
	Wool	Commercial	Z	S	3	Red	Cochineal
	Wool	Raveled	S	Z	2	Red	Cochineal
	Wool	Handspun	Z		1	Red	Aniline
	Wool	Handspun	Z		1	Red	Aniline

14

Blanket
63.34.121

Date: 1860–70
Gift of Mr. and Mrs. Gilbert Maxwell

See Kahlenberg and Berlant 1972:73.

Size: 145.5 cm. x 83 cm.
Count: 13 warps, 46 wefts (handspun), 13 warps, 50 wefts
        (raveled).
Selvage: two cords; 3-ply cochineal dyed red raveled S-Z spin.

	Fiber	*Type of Yarn*	*Spin*	*Twist*	*Ply*	*Color*	*Dye*
Warp	Wool	Handspun	Z		1	White	Natural
	Wool	Handspun	Z		1	Brown	Natural
Weft	Wool	Handspun	Z		1	White	Natural
	Wool	Handspun	Z		1	Blue	Indigo
	Wool	Raveled	Z	S	2	Red	Cochineal
	Wool	Raveled	S	Z	3	Red	Cochineal
	Wool	Handspun	Z		1	Pink	Carded

Note: The 2-ply raveled has larger individual strands than the 3-ply.

15

Blanket
70.65.2

Date: 1875–80
Gift of Dr. Scott Adler

Size: 176 cm. x 125 cm.
Count: 9 warps, 60 wefts.
Selvage: two cords; 2-ply indigo dyed handspun.

	Fiber	Type of Yarn	Spin	Twist	Ply	Color	Dye
Warp	Wool	Handspun	Z		1	White	Natural
Weft	Wool	Handspun	Z		1	White	Natural
	Wool	Handspun	Z		1	Black	Natural+
	Wool	Commercial	Z	S	3	Green	Vegetal
	Wool	Handspun	Z		1	Red/Orange	Aniline
	Wool	Handspun	Z		1	Red/Pink	Cochineal (?)
	Wool	Raveled	S	Z	2	Red/Rose	Cochineal

16

Blanket
63.34.151

Date: 1875–85
Gift of Mr. and Mrs. Gilbert Maxwell

Purchased from Fred Harvey Co.
See Maxwell 1963:34, fig. 19.

Size: 202 cm. x 153 cm.
Count: 15 warps, 64 wefts.
Selvage: two cords; 4-ply aniline dyed black commercial yarn.
A small braided tassel of selvage material is present on either side at approximately the center.

	Fiber	Type of Yarn	Spin	Twist	Ply	Color	Dye
Warp	Wool	Commercial	Z	S	2	White	Natural
Weft	Wool	Commercial	Z	S	2	Black	Aniline
	Wool	Commercial	Z	S	2	Blue	Aniline
	Wool	Commercial	Z	S	3	Red	Aniline
	Wool	Commercial	Z	S	3	White	Natural

17
Blanket
63.34.85

Date: 1875–80
Gift of Mr. and Mrs. Gilbert Maxwell

A so-called slave blanket, woven on a Navajo loom but with a Spanish-American pattern.

Size: 226.5 cm. x 106.5 cm.
Count: 14 warps, 46 wefts.
Selvage: over paired warps, binding stitched on with a sewing
machine.

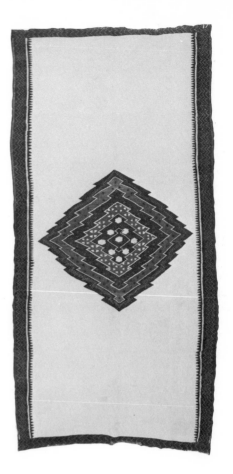

	Fiber	Type of Yarn	Spin	Twist	Ply	Color	Dye
Warp	Wool	Handspun	Z		1	White	Natural
Weft	Wool	Handspun	Z		1	White	Natural
	Wool	Handspun	Z		1	Dark blue	Indigo
	Wool	Handspun	Z		1	Light blue	Indigo
	Wool	Commercial	Z	S	3	Pink	Aniline
	Wool	Commercial	Z	S	3	Yellow	Aniline
	Wool	Commercial	Z	S	3	Green/ Brown	Aniline
	Wool	Commercial	Z	S	3	Pale green	Aniline

Note: The commercial yarn may be an early Germantown.

The Chief's Blanket

The following nine textiles are of the type called "chief's blanket." Their width is always greater than their length, as in Pueblo textiles, and they are characterized by broad horizontal black and white stripes and three patterned bands. In the earliest chief's blankets, the Phase One style, the patterns consists of stripes of red and blue. Phase Two style is recognized by an elaboration of the three bands, generally with bars or ribbonlike designs. Phase Three chief's blankets are the most elaborate with each band containing three serrated or terraced diamonds or triangles.

The chief's style was so popular that it continued to be made as a rug well into the twentieth century and a few are still made today. For this reason the Museum's chief pattern rugs are shown immediately following the classic blanket prototypes. The differences among them are in the materials and fineness of weave rather than in the pattern.

The name presumably came about because these were expensive blankets and an important trade item. Nineteenth-century photographs and drawings demonstrate that chief's blankets were popular among the Plains tribes where they were worn by both men and women. Since there were probably no restrictions on who might wear them, the name used for this design style is certainly meaningless.

18

Blanket, Chief's Pattern, First Phase
63.34.114

Date: 1850–60
Gift of Mr. and Mrs. Gilbert Maxwell

Acquired by Major General F. Funston in 1915.
See Maxwell 1963:11, fig. 2; Kahlenberg and Berlant 1972:17.

Size: 128 cm. x 161 cm.
Count: 10 warps, 56 wefts (handspun) and 10 warps, 64 wefts (raveled).
Selvage: two cords; 3-ply indigo dyed handspun.

	Fiber	Type of Yarn	Spin	Twist	Ply	Color	Dye
Warp	Wool	Handspun	Z		1	White	Natural
Weft	Wool	Handspun	Z		1	White	Natural
	Wool	Handspun	Z		1	Brown	Natural +
	Wool	Raveled	Z	S	2	Red	Cochineal
	Wool	Raveled	Z	S	3	Red	Cochineal

19

Blanket, Chief's Pattern, Second Phase
63.34.113

Date: 1850–60
Gift of Mr. and Mrs. Gilbert Maxwell

See Maxwell 1963:12, fig. 3.

Size: 142 cm. x 183 cm.
Count: 11 warps, 58 wefts.
Selvage: two cords; 3-ply indigo dyed handspun.

	Fiber	Type of Yarn	Spin	Twist	Ply	Color	Dye
Warp	Wool	Handspun	Z		1	White	Natural
Weft	Wool	Handspun	Z		1	Brown	Natural
	Wool	Handspun	Z		1	White	Natural
	Wool	Handspun	Z		1	Blue	Indigo
	Wool	Raveled	S	Z	3	Red	Cochineal

Note: The blue wool is shorter and curlier than that used for other colors.

20

Blanket, Chief's Pattern, Third Phase
63.34.112

Date: 1860–70
Gift of Mr. and Mrs. Gilbert Maxwell

Collected by General O. B. Wilcox in 1870.
See Maxwell 1963:12, fig. 4.

See plate section.

Size: 159 cm. x 182.5 cm.
Count: 12 warps, 52 wefts (handspun) and 12 warps, 60 wefts
(raveled).
Selvage: two cords; 3-ply indigo dyed handspun.

	Fiber	Type of Yarn	Spin	Twist	Ply	Color	Dye
Warp	Wool	Handspun	Z		1	White	Natural
Weft	Wool	Handspun	Z		1	White	Natural
	Wool	Handspun	Z		1	Brown	Natural
	Wool	Handspun	Z		1	Blue	Indigo
	Wool	Handspun	Z		1	Light blue	Indigo
	Wool	Raveled	S	Z	3	Red	Cochineal
	Wool	Raveled	Z	S	2	Red	Cochineal

21

Blanket, Chief's Pattern, Third Phase
63.34.128

Date: ca. 1900

Gift of Mr. and Mrs. Gilbert Maxwell

Purchased by Gilbert Maxwell in 1947
from Annie Wahneka,
Chee Dodge's daughter.

Size: 148 cm. x 233 cm.

Count: 10 warps, 36 wefts (handspun) and 10 warps, 44 wefts (raveled).

Selvage: two cords; 3-ply black aniline dyed handspun.

	Fiber	Type of Yarn	Spin	Twist	Ply	Color	Dye
Warp	Wool	Handspun	Z		1	White	Natural
	Wool	Handspun	Z		1	Dark brown	Natural
Weft	Wool	Handspun	Z		1	Black	Natural+
	Wool	Handspun	Z		1	White	Natural
	Wool	Handspun	Z		1	Purple	Aniline
	Wool	Raveled	Z	S	2	Red	Aniline
	Wool	Commercial	Z	S	4	Red	Aniline

Note: The red commercial red yarn appears only for one inch at one end of the blanket.

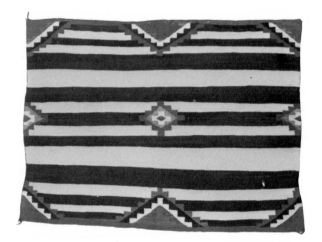

22

Rug, Chief's Pattern, Third Phase
65.47.1

Date: ca. 1934

Gift of Dr. W. W. Hill

Lukachukai.

Size: 125 cm. x 181 cm.

Count: 7 warps, 30 wefts.

Selvage: two cords; 2-ply aniline dyed brown handspun.

	Fiber	Type of Yarn	Spin	Twist	Ply	Color	Dye
Warp	Wool	Handspun	Z		1	White	Natural
Weft	Wool	Handspun	Z		1	White	Natural
	Wool	Handspun	Z		1	Black/ Brown	Natural+
	Wool	Handspun	Z		1	Red	Aniline
	Wool	Handspun	Z		1	Gray	Carded
	Wool	Handspun	Z		1	Med. brown	Aniline

23

Rug, Chief's Pattern, Third Phase
76.1.31

Date: 1900–20
Donor unknown

Size: 147 cm. x 182 cm.
Count: 7 warps, 32 wefts.
Selvage: two cords; 3-ply handspun aniline dyed red.

	Fiber	*Type of Yarn*	*Spin*	*Twist*	*Ply*	*Color*	*Dye*
Warp	Wool	Handspun	Z		1	White	Natural
	Wool	Handspun	Z		1	Brown	Natural
Weft	Wool	Handspun	Z		1	Brown	Natural+
	Wool	Handspun	Z		1	Beige	Carded
	Wool	Handspun	Z		1	White	Natural
	Wool	Handspun	Z		1	Red	Aniline
	Wool	Handspun	Z		1	Orange	Aniline

24

Rug, Fragment of a Chief's Pattern, Third Phase
63.40.2

Date: 1920–40
Gift of Mr. George Johnson

Size: 148 cm. x 114.5 cm.
Count: 6 warps, 22 wefts.
Selvage: two cords; 2-ply natural brown handspun.

	Fiber	*Type of Yarn*	*Spin*	*Twist*	*Ply*	*Color*	*Dye*
Warp	Wool	Handspun	Z		1	White	Natural
Weft	Wool	Handspun	Z		1	White	Natural
	Wool	Handspun	Z		1	Brown	Natural+
	Wool	Handspun	Z		1	Red	Aniline

25

Saddle Blanket, Chief's Pattern
71.9.1

Date: 1940–60

Gift of Mr. Michael Marshall

Size: 69.5 cm. x 87 cm.
Count: 11 warps, 26 wefts.

Selvage: two cords; 3-ply natural brown handspun.

	Fiber	Type of Yarn	Spin	Twist	Ply	Color	Dye
Warp	Wool	Handspun	Z	S	2	Gray	Carded
Weft	Wool	Handspun	Z		1	White	Natural
	Wool	Handspun	Z		1	Black	Aniline
	Wool	Handspun	Z		1	Beige	Carded
	Wool	Handspun	Z		1	Orange	Aniline

26

Rug/Blanket, Chief's Pattern, Second Phase
62.5.1

Date: 1890–1910

Gift of Mrs. Virginia Brockman

Purchased ca. 1910 in New Mexico by D. Brown of Schenectady, N.Y.

Size: 129 cm. x 103 cm.
Count: 7 warps, 20 wefts.

Selvage: two cords; one 2-ply aniline red dyed handspun and the other two 2-ply strands of natural brown handspun which are used side by side and not plied.

	Fiber	Type of Yarn	Spin	Twist	Ply	Color	Dye
Warp	Wool	Handspun	Z		1	White	Natural
	Wool	Handspun	Z		1	Brown	Natural
Weft	Wool	Handspun	Z		1	White	Natural
	Wool	Handspun	Z		1	Black	Aniline (?)
	Wool	Handspun	Z		1	Red	Aniline
	Wool	Handspun	Z		1	Purple	Aniline

Note: Some goat hair carded in.

The Woman's Dress

Before the adoption of white style clothing in the late nineteenth century, the usual dress for a Navajo woman was a two-piece woven garment sewn down the sides and at the shoulders. Each half had the same pattern with a black central portion and red and blue borders at the top and bottom.

A one-piece dress style formerly identified as Pueblo has now been attributed to the Navajo by Dr. Joe Ben Wheat of the University of Colorado. The Museum has four examples of this type of garment (nos. 31–34).

27

Complete Woman's Dress
63.34.145a, b

Date: 1850–60
Gift of Mr. and Mrs. Gilbert Maxwell

Formerly in the Earl Morris Collection. Mr. Morris acquired it in Holbrook, Arizona, in 1928.

Size: 123 cm. x 89.5 cm. and 119.5 cm. x 87 cm.
Count: 13 warps, 60 wefts.
Selvage: two cords; 3-ply indigo dyed handspun.

	Fiber	Type of Yarn	Spin	Twist	Ply	Color	Dye
Warp	Wool	Handspun	Z		1	White	Natural
Weft	Wool	Handspun	Z		1	Black	Natural +
	Wool	Handspun	Z		1	Blue	Indigo
	Wool	Raveled	S	Z	2	Red	Cochineal

28

Complete Woman's Dress
63.34.126

Date: 1880–90
Gift of Mr. and Mrs. Gilbert Maxwell

Registered with the Laboratory of Anthropology, Santa Fe, no. 628.
Formerly in the Maisel and the Earl Morris Collections.
Two halves sewn together at shoulders and down one side.

Size: 126.5 cm. x 81.5 cm. and 128 cm. x 87 cm.

Count: 13 warps, 44 wefts (handspun) and 11 warps, 52 wefts (raveled).

Selvage: two cords; 3-ply indigo dyed handspun.

	Fiber	*Type of Yarn*	*Spin*	*Twist*	*Ply*	*Color*	*Dye*
Warp	Wool	Handspun	Z		1	White	Natural
Weft	Wool	Handspun	Z		1	Black	Natural+
	Wool	Handspun	Z		1	Blue	Indigo
	Wool	Raveled	Z	S	3	Red	Aniline

29

Half of Woman's Dress
73.56.1

Date: 1860–75
Gift of Dr. and Mrs. Lewis Binford

Size: 113 cm. x 80.5 cm.
Count: 14 warps, 60 wefts.
Selvage: two cords; 3-ply indigo dyed handspun.

	Fiber	*Type of Yarn*	*Spin*	*Twist*	*Ply*	*Color*	*Dye*
Warp	Wool	Handspun	Z		1	White	Natural
	Wool	Handspun	Z		1	Brown	Natural
Weft	Wool	Handspun	Z		1	Black	Natural+
	Wool	Handspun	Z		1	Blue	Indigo
	Wool	Raveled	Z	S	2	Red	Cochineal

See plate section.

30

Complete Woman's Dress
63.34.132a, b

Date: 1860–65
Gift of Mr. and Mrs. Gilbert Maxwell

Formerly in the Clay Lockett Collection.

Size: 86 cm. x 123 cm. and 90 cm. x 140 cm.
Count: 13 warps, 44 wefts.
Selvage: two cords; 2-ply indigo dyed handspun.

	Fiber	Type of Yarn	Spin	Twist	Ply	Color	Dye
Warp	Wool	Handspun	Z		1	White	Natural
Weft	Wool	Handspun	Z		1	Black	Natural+
	Wool	Handspun	Z		1	Blue	Indigo
	Wool	Raveled	S	Z	2	Red	Aniline

31

Woman's Dress
63.34.133

Date: 1900–10
Gift of Mr. and Mrs. Gilbert Maxwell

Bought in Shiprock in 1910 by Earl Morris.
Twill weave.

Size: 129 cm. x 163 cm.
Selvage: two cords; 3-ply black dyed handspun.

	Fiber	Type of Yarn	Spin	Twist	Ply	Color	Dye
Warp	Cotton	String				White	Natural
Weft	Wool	Handspun	Z		1	Black	Natural & aniline
	Wool	Handspun	Z		1	Gray/Brown	Aniline
	Wool	Handspun	Z		1	Red	Aniline

32

Woman's Dress
63.34.138
Date: ca. 1880
Gift of Mr. and Mrs. Gilbert Maxwell
Twill weave.
Size: 107 cm. x 140 cm.

Selvage: two cords; 3-ply indigo dyed handspun.

	Fiber	Type of Yarn	Spin	Twist	Ply	Color	Dye
Warp	Wool	Handspun	Z		1	Brown	Natural
Weft	Wool	Handspun	Z		1	Black	Natural +
	Wool	Handspun	Z		1	Blue	Indigo
	Wool	Raveled	Z	S	2	Red	Cochineal

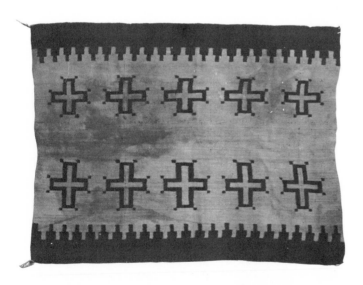

33

Woman's Dress
63.34.130
Date: 1880–90
Gift of Mr. and Mrs. Gilbert Maxwell

Plain twill weave with areas of diamond and herringbone.
Size: 110.5 cm. x 152 cm.
Selvage: two cords; 3-ply aniline red dyed handspun.

	Fiber	Type of Yarn	Spin	Twist	Ply	Color	Dye
Warp	Wool	Handspun	Z		1	Brown	Natural
Weft	Wool	Handspun	Z		1	Black	Aniline (?)
	Wool	Handspun	Z		1	Blue	Indigo
	Wool	Raveled	S	Z	3	Red	Cochineal

34

Woman's Dress
63.15.5

Date: 1875–80
Purchase

Plain twill weave with areas of herringbone twill.

Size: 103 cm. x 140 cm.
Selvage: two cords; 3-ply indigo dyed handspun. Break in the
cords halfway down.

	Fiber	Type of Yarn	Spin	Twist	Ply	Color	Dye
Warp	Wool	Handspun	Z		1	Brown	Natural
Weft	Wool	Handspun	Z		1	Red	Aniline
	Wool	Handspun	Z		1	Black	Natural+
	Wool	Handspun	Z		1	Blue	Indigo

Eyedazzlers (ca. 1880–ca. 1900)

In the last quarter of the nineteenth century Navajo weaving underwent an important change. The arrival of the railroad in the Southwest in 1880–81 brought a flood of manufactured goods from the East. Up to this time, Indians (Ute and Cheyenne as well as Navajo) had been the principal users of Navajo weaving. With cheap industrially made cloth and clothing now available there was no longer a need for the fine waterproof handwoven blankets and dresses. Weavers had to find new markets and new uses for their products. In addition, packaged aniline dyes and commercially spun aniline dyed yarn called "Germantown" (from a town in Pennsylvania, now part of Philadelphia) were also imported. The new wide range of bright colors led to experimentation with bold color combinations, hence the derogatory term "eyedazzler" for weaving of this period.

Some weavers were encouraged by white traders to make textiles suitable for use as floor coverings. These were heavier and coarser than blankets and, ultimately, had radically different patterns. Borders were added, cautiously at first, with narrow bands at the top and bottom, and later on all four sides. Large central motifs and vertical patterning replaced the predominantly horizontal orientation of the classic period blankets. Although some Navajo wove blankets for their own use until about 1900, items made for use in white homes—pillow covers, table top runners—as well as rugs came to dominate the Navajo weaving industry. The simple striped blanket continued to be made, but it became increasingly coarse and colored with aniline dyes. Germantown yarn was more expensive than home-dyed handspun and the traders saved it for the better weavers. Consequently Germantown textiles of this period tend to be technically superior to contemporary handspun ones.

The classic weaving style did not come to a sudden end with the introduction of aniline dyes. The first four blankets in this section are entirely classic in their patterning and character, only the use of the new materials places them in this later period.

35

Blanket
63.34.73

Date: 1880–85
Gift of Mr. and Mrs. Gilbert Maxwell

Formerly in the Earl Morris Collection. Purchased from F. M. Pierce who acquired it in Farmington in 1890.

Size: 180 cm. x 124 cm.
Count: 9 warps, 32 wefts.
Selvage: two cords; 2-ply aniline dyed orange handspun.

	Fiber	Type of Yarn	Spin	Twist	Ply	Color	Dye
Warp	Cotton	String				White	Natural
Weft	Wool	Handspun	Z		1	Orange	Aniline
	Wool	Handspun	Z		1	Green	Aniline
	Wool	Handspun	Z		1	Blue	Indigo
	Wool	Handspun	Z		1	Red	Aniline
	Wool	Handspun	Z		1	White	Natural
	Wool	Handspun	Z		1	Pink	Carded

36

Blanket, Woman's Style
63.34.140

Date: 1875–80
Gift of Mr. and Mrs. Gilbert Maxwell

This type of blanket with narrow brown and beige stripes and three bands of pattern running horizontally is the equivalent to the chief's blanket for women.
See Maxwell 1963:13, fig. 5.

Size: 110.5 cm. x 144.5 cm.
Count: 8 warps, 32 wefts.
Selvage: completely redone.

	Fiber	Type of Yarn	Spin	Twist	Ply	Color	Dye
Warp	Wool	Handspun	Z		1	White	Natural
Weft	Wool	Handspun	Z		1	Dark brown	Natural+
	Wool	Handspun	Z		1	Light brown	Carded
	Wool	Handspun	Z		1	Blue	Indigo
	Wool	Handspun	Z		1	Yellow	Vegetal (?)
	Wool	Handspun	Z		1	Red	Aniline

37

Blanket
64.26.2

Date: 1880–90
Gift of Mr. Read Mullan

Size: 192 cm. x 131 cm.
Count: 7 warps, 26 wefts.
Selvage: completely redone.

	Fiber	Type of Yarn	Spin	Twist	Ply	Color	Dye
Warp	Wool	Handspun	Z		1	White	Natural
Weft	Wool	Handspun	Z		1	White	Natural
	Wool	Handspun	Z		1	Orange	Aniline
	Wool	Handspun	Z		1	Yellow	Aniline
	Wool	Handspun	Z		1	Black	Aniline
	Wool	Handspun	Z		1	Green	Aniline
	Wool	Handspun	Z		1	Red/Orange	Aniline

38

Rug/Blanket
72.31.1

Date: 1880–90
Gift of Mr. Charles B. Popkin

Size: 189 cm. x 128 cm.
Count: 9 warps, 32 wefts.
Selvage: two cords; 2-ply aniline red dyed handspun.

	Fiber	Type of Yarn	Spin	Twist	Ply	Color	Dye
Warp	Wool	Handspun	Z		1	White	Natural
Weft	Wool	Handspun	Z		1	White	Natural
	Wool	Handspun	Z		1	Red/Orange	Aniline
	Wool	Handspun	Z		1	Dark yellow	Aniline
	Wool	Handspun	Z		1	Light yellow	Aniline
	Wool	Handspun	Z		1	Green	Indigo & yellow

Note: The yellows are faded and now appear greenish.

39

Blanket
63.34.125

Date: 1880–95
Gift of Mr. and Mrs. Gilbert Maxwell
See Maxwell 1963:33, fig. 17.
Purchased in 1895 by Earl Morris.

Size: 211 cm. x 126 cm.
Count: 10 warps, 26 wefts (handspun) and 10 warps, 30 wefts (commercial).
Selvage: two cords; 3-ply aniline dyed orange handspun.

	Fiber	Type of Yarn	Spin	Twist	Ply	Color	Dye
Warp	Wool	Handspun	Z		1	White	Natural
Weft	Wool	Handspun	Z		1	Orange	Aniline
	Wool	Handspun	Z		1	White	Natural
	Wool	Handspun	Z		1	Yellow	Aniline
	Wool	Handspun	Z		1	Red	Aniline
	Wool	Commercial	Z	S	4	Green	Aniline
	Wool	Commercial	Z	S	4	Purple	Aniline
	Wool	Commercial	Z	S	4	Yellow (faded)	Aniline

Note: The yellow commercial yarn appears in the center only.

40

Rug/Blanket
63.34.99

Date: 1885–95
Gift of Mr. and Mrs. Gilbert Maxwell

Size: 160 cm. x 139 cm.
Count: 4 warps, 16 wefts.
Selvage: two cords; each 2-ply aniline dyed red handspun.

	Fiber	Type of Yarn	Spin	Twist	Ply	Color	Dye
Warp	Wool	Handspun	Z		1	White	Natural
Weft	Wool	Handspun	Z		1	Red	Aniline
	Wool	Handspun	Z		1	White	Natural
	Wool	Handspun	Z		1	Brown	Natural+
	Wool	Handspun	Z		1	Orange	Aniline

See plate section.

41

Blanket
63.34.176

Date: 1880–90
Gift of Mr. and Mrs. Gilbert Maxwell

Formerly in the Earl Morris Collection.
Size: 177 cm. x 127 cm.
Count: 8 warps, 24 wefts.
Selvage: two cords; 2-ply aniline dyed orange handspun.

	Fiber	Type of Yarn	Spin	Twist	Ply	Color	Dye
Warp	Wool	Handspun	Z		1	White	Natural
Weft	Wool	Handspun	Z		1	Orange	Aniline
	Wool	Handspun	Z		1	Blue	Aniline
	Wool	Handspun	Z		1	Yellow	Aniline
	Wool	Handspun	Z		1	Black	Aniline
	Wool	Handspun	Z		1	Light green	Aniline
	Wool	Handspun	Z		1	White	Natural

42

Rug
74.27.1

Date: 1880–90
Gift of Mrs. C. W. Franklin

Size: 138 cm. x 83 cm.
Count: 6 warps, 30 wefts.
Selvage: two cords; 2-ply aniline dyed handspun—one red and
one green plied together.

	Fiber	Type of Yarn	Spin	Twist	Ply	Color	Dye
Warp	Wool	Handspun	Z		1	Black	Aniline
Weft	Wool	Handspun	Z		1	Black	Aniline
	Wool	Handspun	Z		1	Red	Aniline
	Wool	Handspun	Z		1	Orange	Aniline
	Wool	Handspun	Z		1	Green	Aniline

43

Blanket
63.34.118

Date: 1875–80
Gift of Mr. and Mrs. Gilbert Maxwell

Formerly in Earl Morris Collection.

Size: 120 cm. x 78.5 cm.
Count: 8 warps, 48 wefts.
Selvage: two cords; 3-ply indigo dyed handspun.

	Fiber	Type of Yarn	Spin	Twist	Ply	Color	Dye
Warp	Wool	Handspun	Z		1	White	Natural
Weft	Wool	Handspun	Z		1	Blue	Indigo
	Wool	Commercial	Z	S	3	Green	Aniline (?)
	Wool	Commercial	Z	S	3	Yellow	Aniline (?)
	Wool	Raveled	Z	S	2	Red/Orange	Aniline

44

Blanket
63.34.160

Date: ca. 1890
Gift of Mr. and Mrs. Gilbert Maxwell

Formerly in the Earl Morris Collection.

Size: 124 cm. x 29.5 cm.
Count: 10 warps, 54 wefts.
Selvage: appears to be completely redone.

	Fiber	Type of Yarn	Spin	Twist	Ply	Color	Dye
Warp	Wool	Commercial	Z	S	4	Brown	Aniline
	Wool	Commercial	Z	S	4	White	Aniline
	Wool	Commercial	Z	S	4	Green	Aniline
Weft	Wool	Commercial	Z	S	4	White	Aniline
	Wool	Commercial	Z	S	4	Green (2 shades)	Aniline
	Wool	Commercial	Z	S	4	Purple	Aniline
	Wool	Commercial	Z	S	4	Red	Aniline
	Wool	Commercial	Z	S	4	Brown	Aniline
	Wool	Commercial	Z	S	4	Black	Aniline
	Wool	Commercial	Z	S	4	Yellow	Aniline

Note: Warps are not continuous at one end, but are cut and doubled back
into the fabric.

45

Blanket
63.34.147

Date: 1890–1900
Gift of Mr. and Mrs. Gilbert Maxwell

Size: 122 cm. x 91 cm.
Count: 8 warps, 40 wefts.
Selvage: two cords; 3-ply, each ply made of a strand of 4-ply
salt-and-pepper yarn and two strands of red yarn.

	Fiber	Type of Yarn	Spin	Twist	Ply	Color	Dye
Warp	Cotton	String				White	Natural
Weft	Wool	Commercial	Z	S	4	White	Natural
	Wool	Commercial	Z	S	4	Black	Aniline
	Wool	Commercial	Z	S	4	Brown	Aniline
	Wool	Commercial	Z	S	4	Maroon	Aniline
	Wool	Commercial	Z	S	4	Red	Aniline
	Wool	Commercial	Z	S	4	Salt & pepper	Aniline

Note: Salt-and-pepper yarn is tie-dyed.

46

Rug
53.10.1

Date: 1890–1900
Gift of Mr. Irving D. Townsend

Size: 200 cm. x 123.5 cm.
Count: 5 warps, 16 wefts.
Selvage: no cord, over two warps.

	Fiber	Type of Yarn	Spin	Twist	Ply	Color	Dye
Warp	Wool	Handspun	Z		1	White	Natural
	Wool	Handspun	Z		1	Brown	Natural
Weft	Wool	Handspun	Z		1	White	Natural
	Wool	Handspun	Z		1	Brown	Natural+
	Wool	Handspun	Z		1	Light brown	Carded
	Wool	Handspun	Z		1	Orange	Aniline
	Wool	Handspun	Z		1	Yellow	Aniline

47

Blanket/Rug
65.43.1

Date: 1885–95
Gift of Mrs. Loretta Dohner

Size: 178.5 cm. x 121.5 cm.
Count: 6 warps, 24 wefts.
Selvage: completely missing.

	Fiber	Type of Yarn	Spin	Twist	Ply	Color	Dye
Warp	Wool	Handspun	Z		1	White	Natural
Weft	Wool	Handspun	Z		1	Brown	Natural
	Wool	Handspun	Z		1	Beige	Carded
	Wool	Handspun	Z		1	Red	Aniline
	Wool	Handspun	Z		1	Green	Aniline
	Wool	Handspun	Z		1	Yellow	Aniline

48

Blanket
63.34.159

Date: 1880–90
Gift of Mr. and Mrs. Gilbert Maxwell

Size: 111 cm. x 75.5 cm.
Count: 12 warps, 40 wefts.
Selvage: missing, bound top and bottom with cloth.

	Fiber	Type of Yarn	Spin	Twist	Ply	Color	Dye
Warp	Wool	Commercial	Z	S	4	Yellow	Aniline
Weft	Wool	Commercial	Z	S	4	White	Aniline
	Wool	Commercial	Z	S	4	Gold	Aniline
	Wool	Commercial	Z	S	4	Blue/Green	Aniline
	Wool	Commercial	Z	S	4	Olive green	Aniline
	Wool	Commercial	Z	S	4	Red	Aniline

49

Saddle Blanket
75.329.1

Date: 1880–1900
Gift of Mrs. Maurine Grammer

Size: 74 cm. x 67 cm.
Count: 12 warps, 48 wefts.
Selvage: three cords; each two strands of 4-ply aniline dyed
    pink yarn.

	Fiber	Type of Yarn	Spin	Twist	Ply	Color	Dye
Warp	Wool	Handspun	Z		1	White	Natural
Weft	Wool	Commercial	Z	S	4	Maroon	Aniline
	Wool	Commercial	Z	S	4	Gold	Aniline
	Wool	Commercial	Z	S	4	Yellow	Aniline
	Wool	Commercial	Z	S	4	Purple	Aniline
	Wool	Commercial	Z	S	4	Gray	Aniline
	Wool	Commercial	Z	S	4	Turquoise	Aniline
	Wool	Commercial	Z	S	4	Salt & pepper	Aniline

50

Blanket
63.34.173

Date: 1885–93

Gift of Mr. and Mrs. Gilbert Maxwell

Collected originally in New Mexico between 1888 and 1893.

Size: 160.5 cm. x 119.5 cm.

Count: 7 warps, 32 wefts.

Selvage: two cords; one orange and one black. Both 3-ply aniline dyed handspun.

	Fiber	Type of Yarn	Spin	Twist	Ply	Color	Dye
Warp	Wool	Handspun	Z		1	White	Natural
Weft	Wool	Handspun	Z		1	White	Natural
	Wool	Handspun	Z		1	Black	Aniline (?)
	Wool	Handspun	Z		1	Orange	Aniline
	Wool	Handspun	Z		1	Red	Aniline

51

Rug/Blanket
65.57.13

Date: 1890–1900

Gift of Mr. Raymond Jonson,
Vera Jonson Memorial Collection

Size: 194.5 cm. x 124.5 cm.

Count: 6 warps, 24 wefts.

Selvage: two cords; 2-ply natural white handspun.

	Fiber	Type of Yarn	Spin	Twist	Ply	Color	Dye
Warp	Wool	Handspun	Z		1	White	Natural
Weft	Wool	Handspun	Z		1	White	Natural
	Wool	Handspun	Z		1	Dark brown	Natural+
	Wool	Handspun	Z		1	Gray	Carded
	Wool	Handspun	Z		1	Red	Aniline
	Wool	Handspun	Z		1	Purple	Aniline
	Wool	Handspun	Z		1	Lavender (faded)	Carded

52

Rug/Blanket
67.123.2

Date: 1890–1900
Gift of Mrs. Leigh E. Smith in
memory of Mary Augustus Brown

Size: 264 cm. x 150.5 cm.
Count: 7 warps, 14 wefts.
Selvage: two cords; 2-ply carded beige handspun.

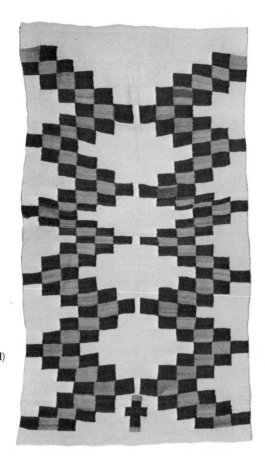

	Fiber	Type of Yarn	Spin	Twist	Ply	Color	Dye
Warp	Cotton	String				White	Natural
Weft	Wool	Handspun	Z		1	White	Natural
	Wool	Handspun	Z		1	Brown	Natural
	Wool	Handspun	Z		1	Gold	Vegetal
	Wool	Handspun	Z		1	Rust/Pink	Carded (White & aniline red)

Note: Goat hair carded in.

53

Blanket
63.34.111

Date: 1880–1900
Gift of Mr. and Mrs. Gilbert Maxwell

Formerly in the Earl Morris Collection.
Pulled warp or wedge weave.
See Maxwell 1963:41, fig. 41.

Size: 171.5 cm. x 132 cm.
Count: 6 warps, 34 wefts.
Selvage: two cords; 3-ply aniline dyed orange handspun.

	Fiber	Type of Yarn	Spin	Twist	Ply	Color	Dye
Warp	Wool	Handspun	Z		1	White	Natural
Weft	Wool	Handspun	Z		1	White	Natural
	Wool	Handspun	Z		1	Brown	Natural
	Wool	Handspun	Z		1	Orange	Aniline
	Wool	Handspun	Z		1	Yellow	Aniline
	Wool	Handspun	Z		1	Beige	Carded
	Wool	Handspun	Z		1	Rust/Pink	Aniline

54

Rug/Blanket
63.33.6

Date: 1880–1900
Gift of Mrs. Gilbert Milne

Size: 187 cm. x 141.5 cm.
Count: 5 warps, 16 wefts.
Selvage: two cords; 2-ply natural white handspun.

	Fiber	Type of Yarn	Spin	Twist	Ply	Color	Dye
Warp	Wool	Handspun	Z		1	White	Natural
Weft	Wool	Handspun	Z		1	White	Natural
	Wool	Handspun	Z		1	Brown	Natural+
	Wool	Handspun	Z		1	Red	Aniline
	Wool	Handspun	Z		1	Pink	Aniline
	Wool	Handspun	Z		1	Orange	Aniline
	Wool	Handspun	Z		1	Yellow	Aniline

55

Rug/Blanket
71.29.1

Date: 1890–1900
Gift of Mr. and Mrs. William K. McNaught

Size: 227 cm. x 120 cm.
Count: 5 warps, 20 wefts.
Selvage: two cords; 2-ply aniline dyed red handspun.

	Fiber	Type of Yarn	Spin	Twist	Ply	Color	Dye
Warp	Wool	Handspun	Z		1	White	Natural
	Wool	Handspun	Z		1	Brown	Natural
Weft	Wool	Handspun	Z		1	White	Natural
	Wool	Handspun	Z		1	Black	Aniline
	Wool	Handspun	Z		1	Red	Aniline
	Wool	Handspun	Z		1	Orange	Aniline

56

Blanket
68.1.17

Date: 1890–1900
Donor unknown

Size: 74 cm. x 72.5 cm.
Count: 10 warps, 48 wefts.
Selvage: two cords; 4-ply aniline dyed russet commercial yarn.

	Fiber	Type of Yarn	Spin	Twist	Ply	Color	Dye
Warp	Cotton	String				White	Natural
Weft	Wool	Commercial	Z	S	4	Dark red	Aniline
	Wool	Commercial	Z	S	4	Light red	Aniline
	Wool	Commercial	Z	S	4	Green	Aniline
	Wool	Commercial	Z	S	4	Russet	Aniline
	Wool	Commercial	Z	S	4	Beige	Aniline

57

Blanket
74.28.2

Date: 1885–95
Donor unknown

Size: 131.5 cm. x 81.5 cm.
Count: 9 warps, 56 wefts.
Selvage: two cords; 3-ply composed of three strands of 4-ply maroon aniline dyed commercial yarn.

	Fiber	Type of Yarn	Spin	Twist	Ply	Color	Dye
Warp	Cotton	String				White	Natural
Weft	Wool	Commercial	Z	S	4	White	Natural
	Wool	Commercial	Z	S	4	Maroon	Aniline
	Wool	Commercial	Z	S	4	Red	Aniline
	Wool	Commercial	Z	S	4	Green	Aniline
	Wool	Commercial	Z	S	4	Purple (2 shades)	Aniline

58

Rug

70.65.3

Date: 1880–1900

Gift of Dr. Scott Adler

Size: 192.5 cm. x 154 cm.

Count: 8 warps, 44 wefts.

Selvage: completely redone.

	Fiber	Type of Yarn	Spin	Twist	Ply	Color	Dye
Warp	Wool	Commercial	Z	S	2	Red	Aniline
Weft	Wool	Commercial	Z	S	4	Black	Aniline
	Wool	Commercial	Z	S	4	White	Aniline
	Wool	Commercial	Z	S	4	Salt & pepper	Aniline
	Wool	Commercial	Z	S	4	Red	Aniline
	Wool	Commercial	Z	S	4	Orange	Aniline

Note: Salt-and-pepper yarn appears to be tie-dyed.

59

Saddle Blanket

73.26.2

Date: 1900–23

Gift of Dr. Andrew C. Bratton

Formerly in the Ethel Mae Bratton Collection.

Exhibited at First National Intertribal Indian Ceremonial at Gallup, N.M., in 1923 by C. N. Cotton. It won the first prize for weaving.

Size: 143 cm. x 87 cm.

Count: 11 warps, 42 wefts.

Selvage: two cords; 4-ply aniline dyed red commercial yarn.

	Fiber	Type of Yarn	Spin	Twist	Ply	Color	Dye
Warp	Cotton	String				White	Natural
Weft	Wool	Commercial	Z	S	4	Red	Aniline
	Wool	Commercial	Z	S	4	Maroon	Aniline
	Wool	Commercial	Z	S	4	Black	Aniline
	Wool	Commercial	Z	S	4	White	Aniline
	Wool	Commercial	Z	S	4	Yellow	Aniline
	Wool	Commercial	Z	S	4	Purple	Aniline
	Wool	Commercial	Z	S	4	Green	Aniline

See plate section.

60

Saddle Blanket
63.34.158

Date: 1885–95

Gift of Mr. and Mrs. Gilbert Maxwell

Purchased in Carlsbad in 1945.
Fringe of 4-ply commercial yarn aniline dyed red, purple, and white.

Size: 118 cm. x 80.5 cm.
Count: 10 warps, 46 wefts.
Selvage: two cords; 2-ply with each ply one strand of 4-ply aniline dyed red commercial yarn.

	Fiber	Type of Yarn	Spin	Twist	Ply	Color	Dye
Warp	Cotton	String				White	Natural
Weft	Wool	Commercial	Z	S	4	Purple	Aniline
	Wool	Commercial	Z	S	4	Red	Aniline
	Wool	Commercial	Z	S	4	White	Natural

61

Rug
67.14.2

Date: 1890–1900
Purchase

Size: 187.5 cm. x 120 cm.
Count: 12 warps, 44 wefts.
Selvage: two cords; 2-ply aniline dyed orange handspun.

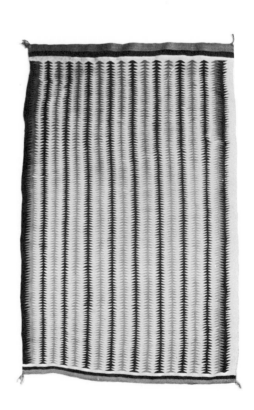

	Fiber	Type of Yarn	Spin	Twist	Ply	Color	Dye
Warp	Cotton	String				White	Natural
Weft	Wool	Handspun	Z		1	White	Natural
	Wool	Handspun	Z		1	Orange	Aniline
	Wool	Handspun	Z		1	Black	Aniline

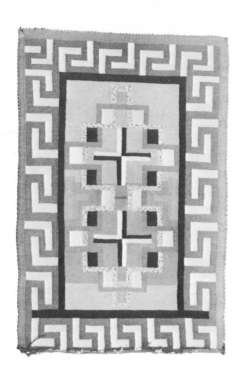

62

Rug
65.65.2

Date: 1880–1900

Gift of A. Margaret Anson

Size: 87.5 cm. x 59 cm.

Count: 12 warps, 50 wefts.

Selvage: two cords; 4-ply aniline dyed commercial yarn, one gold, one black.

	Fiber	Type of Yarn	Spin	Twist	Ply	Color	Dye
Warp	Cotton	String				White	Natural
Weft	Wool	Commercial	Z	S	4	Red	Aniline
	Wool	Commercial	Z	S	4	Black	Aniline
	Wool	Commercial	Z	S	4	White	Natural
	Wool	Commercial	Z	S	4	Green	Aniline
	Wool	Commercial	Z	S	4	Yellow	Aniline
	Wool	Commercial	Z	S	4	Pink	Aniline
	Wool	Commercial	Z	S	4	Russet	Aniline
	Wool	Commercial	Z	S	4	Olive salt & pepper	Aniline

Note: Salt-and-pepper yarn is tie-dyed.

63

Saddle Blanket
63.34.144

Date: 1880–90

Gift of Mr. and Mrs. Gilbert Maxwell

Formerly in the Andrus Collection.

Size: 95.5 cm. x 75 cm.

Count: 8 warps, 40 wefts.

Selvage: two cords; 2-ply aniline dyed purple handspun.

	Fiber	Type of Yarn	Spin	Twist	Ply	Color	Dye
Warp	Cotton	String				White	Natural
Weft	Wool	Commercial	Z	S	4	White	Natural
	Wool	Commercial	Z	S	4	Green	Aniline
	Wool	Commercial	Z	S	4	Yellow	Aniline
	Wool	Commercial	Z	S	4	Black	Aniline

64

Rug
63.34.182

Date: 1885–1900

Gift of Mr. and Mrs. Gilbert Maxwell

Purchased from Clay Lockett in 1948.

Size: 128 cm. x 86 cm.

Count: 9 warps, 47 wefts.

Selvage: three cords; each two strands of 4-ply aniline dyed black commercial yarn.

	Fiber	Type of Yarn	Spin	Twist	Ply	Color	Dye
Warp	Cotton	String				White	Natural
Weft	Wool	Commercial	Z	S	4	Red	Aniline
	Wool	Commercial	Z	S	4	Black	Aniline
	Wool	Commercial	Z	S	4	Green	Aniline
	Wool	Handspun	Z		1	White	Natural

65

Pillow Cover
65.65.1

Date: 1890–1900

Gift of A. Margaret Anson

Size: 52.5 cm. x 55.5 cm.

Count: 10 warps, 48 wefts.

Selvage: two cords; each two 4-ply strands of aniline dyed blue commercial yarn.

	Fiber	Type of Yarn	Spin	Twist	Ply	Color	Dye
Warp	Cotton	String				White	Natural
Weft	Wool	Commercial	Z	S	4	Red	Aniline
	Wool	Commercial	Z	S	4	Purple	Aniline
	Wool	Commercial	Z	S	4	Maroon	Aniline
	Wool	Commercial	Z	S	4	Orange	Aniline
	Wool	Commercial	Z	S	4	Green	Aniline
	Wool	Commercial	Z	S	4	Yellow/ Green	Aniline
	Wool	Commercial	Z	S	4	White	Natural
	Wool	Commercial	Z	S	4	Pink	Aniline

66

Rug/Blanket
64.26.1

Date: 1885–95
Gift of Mr. Read Mullan

Size: 198 cm. x 126 cm.
Count: 9 warps, 26 wefts.
Selvage: two cords; 2-ply aniline dyed red handspun.

	Fiber	Type of Yarn	Spin	Twist	Ply	Color	Dye
Warp	Wool	Handspun	Z		1	White	Natural
Weft	Wool	Handspun	Z		1	White	Natural
	Wool	Handspun	Z		1	Orange	Aniline
	Wool	Handspun	Z		1	Yellow	Aniline
	Wool	Handspun	Z		1	Green	Aniline
	Wool	Handspun	Z		1	Blue	Indigo

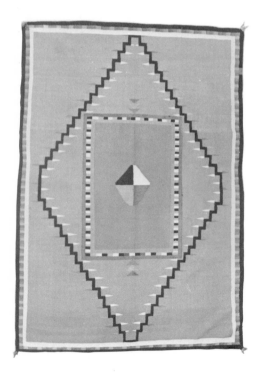

67

Rug
63.34.109

Date: 1885–95
Gift of Mr. and Mrs. Gilbert Maxwell
See Maxwell 1963:33, fig. 18.

Size: 196 cm. x 144 cm.
Count: 9 warps, 44 wefts.
Selvage: two cords; 4-ply aniline dyed red yarn.

	Fiber	Type of Yarn	Spin	Twist	Ply	Color	Dye
Warp	Wool	Commercial	Z	S	2	White	Natural
Weft	Wool	Commercial	Z	S	4	White	Natural
	Wool	Commercial	Z	S	4	Red	Aniline
						(2 shades)	
	Wool	Commercial	Z	S	4	Purple	Aniline
	Wool	Commercial	Z	S	4	Black	Aniline
	Wool	Commercial	Z	S	4	Green	Aniline

8. Navajo blanket

11. Navajo blanket

13. Navajo blanket

20. Navajo blanket

29. Navajo woman's dress

40. Navajo rug/blanket

59. Navajo saddle blanket

68. Navajo rug

68

Rug
63.34.149

Date: 1880–90
Gift of Mr. and Mrs. Gilbert Maxwell

Size: 344 cm. x 328.5 cm.
Count: 11 warps, 52 wefts.
Selvage: completely redone.

	Fiber	*Type of Yarn*	*Spin*	*Twist*	*Ply*	*Color*	*Dye*
Warp	Cotton	String				White	Natural
Weft	Wool	Commercial	Z	S	4	White	Natural
	Wool	Commercial	Z	S	4	Red/Orange	Aniline
	Wool	Commercial	Z	S	4	Maroon	Aniline
	Wool	Commercial	Z	S	4	Yellow	Aniline
	Wool	Commercial	Z	S	4	Green	Aniline
	Wool	Commercial	Z	S	4	Black	Aniline
	Wool	Commercial	Z	S	4	Purple	Aniline
	Wool	Commercial	Z	S	3	Light blue	Aniline
	Wool	Commercial	Z	S	3	Med. blue	Aniline
	Wool	Commercial	Z	S	3	Dark blue	Aniline

Note: Warps are cut at top and bottom and tucked back in for about one inch.

See plate section.

69

Rug/Blanket
65.46.2

Date: 1890–1910
Gift of Mrs. W. H. Loerpabel

Size: 186.5 cm. x 111.5 cm.
Count: 8 warps, 20 wefts.
Selvage: two cords; 3-ply natural white handspun.

	Fiber	*Type of Yarn*	*Spin*	*Twist*	*Ply*	*Color*	*Dye*
Warp	Wool	Handspun	Z		1	White	Natural
Weft	Wool	Handspun	Z		1	White	Natural
	Wool	Handspun	Z		1	Brown	Natural+
	Wool	Handspun	Z		1	Blue	Indigo
	Wool	Handspun	Z		1	Green	Indigo & yellow
	Wool	Handspun	Z		1	Pink	Aniline (?)

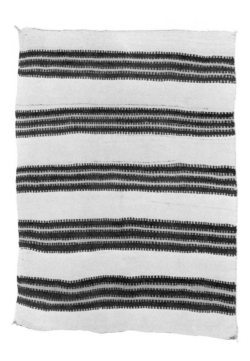

70

Blanket

63.34.117

Date: 1880–1900

Gift of Mr. and Mrs. Gilbert Maxwell

Purchased from Maisel Collection in 1944. Registered with Laboratory of Anthropology, Santa Fe, no. 647.

Size: 166 cm. x 121 cm.

Count: 4 warps, 16 wefts.

Selvage: two cords; 2-ply handspun (one pink, one yellow aniline dyed).

	Fiber	Type of Yarn	Spin	Twist	Ply	Color	Dye
Warp	Wool	Handspun	Z		1	Brown	Natural
Weft	Wool	Handspun	Z		1	White	Natural
	Wool	Handspun	Z		1	White	Natural
	Wool	Handspun	Z		1	Brown	Natural
	Wool	Handspun	Z		1	Pink	Aniline

71

Blanket

63.34.174

Date: 1885–95

Gift of Mr. and Mrs. Gilbert Maxwell

Purchased from Carlsbad Caverns Supply Co. in 1946. Registered with Laboratory of Anthropology, Santa Fe, no. 644.

Size: 176 cm. x 126 cm.

Count: 7 warps, 30 wefts.

Selvage: two cords; 3-ply aniline dyed orange handspun.

	Fiber	Type of Yarn	Spin	Twist	Ply	Color	Dye
Warp	Wool	Handspun	Z		1	White	Natural
Weft	Wool	Handspun	Z		1	Orange	Aniline
	Wool	Handspun	Z		1	Pink	Carded
	Wool	Handspun	Z		1	Brown	Natural
	Wool	Handspun	Z		1	Yellow	Aniline

Note: Warp is cut into fringe and knotted.

72

Blanket
66.113.2

Date: 1890–1900
Gift of Mrs. Prudence E. Oakes

Size: 155 cm. x 120 cm.
Count: 6 warps, 16 wefts.
Selvage: two cords; 2-ply handspun (one natural brown and one aniline dyed red).

	Fiber	Type of Yarn	Spin	Twist	Ply	Color	Dye
Warp	Wool	Handspun	Z		1	White	Natural
	Wool	Handspun	Z		1	Gray	Carded
Weft	Wool	Handspun	Z		1	White	Natural
	Wool	Handspun	Z		1	Black	Aniline
	Wool	Handspun	Z		1	Red	Aniline
	Wool	Handspun	Z		1	Orange	Aniline
	Wool	Handspun	Z		1	Yellow	Aniline
	Wool	Handspun	Z		1	Dark blue	Aniline
	Wool	Handspun	Z		1	Med. blue	Aniline
	Wool	Handspun	Z		1	Pink	Aniline
	Wool	Handspun	Z		1	Pink & brown	Carded

73

Rug
66.113.4

Date: 1890–1900
Gift of Mrs. Prudence E. Oakes

Size: 153 cm. x 82 cm.
Count: 8 warps, 24 wefts.
Selvage: two cords; 2-ply carded beige handspun.

	Fiber	Type of Yarn	Spin	Twist	Ply	Color	Dye
Warp	Wool	Handspun	Z		1	White	Natural
Weft	Wool	Handspun	Z		1	White	Natural
	Wool	Handspun	Z		1	Dark brown	Natural+
	Wool	Handspun	Z		1	Gray	Aniline
	Wool	Handspun	Z		1	Red	Aniline

74

Table Runner
55.20.26

Date: 1895–1900
Gift of Mrs. Richard Wetherill

From Mrs. Wetherill's notes: "The bayetta in this blanket was some that was manufactured in Boston. It was an experiment and while a good copy, it faded. We never handled it at our trading post, but Horbin at Thoreau has some. One of our Navaho women bought two yards for a dress, but her husband made her weave this blanket."

Size: 168 cm. x 36.5 cm.
Count: 12 warps, 34 wefts.
Selvage: completely redone.

	Fiber	Type of Yarn	Spin	Twist	Ply	Color	Dye
Warp	Wool	Handspun	Z		1	White	Natural
Weft	Wool	Handspun	Z		1	White	Natural
	Wool	Handspun	Z		1	Gray (faded purple)	Aniline
	Wool	Raveled	S	Z	3	Red	Cochineal (?)

75

Table Runner
55.20.28

Date: 1895–1902
Gift of Mrs. Richard Wetherill

Purchased in 1902 in El Paso, Texas.

Size: 131 cm. x 29 cm.
Count: 12 warps, 60 wefts.
Selvage: two cords; each two strands of single-ply aniline red dyed handspun.

	Fiber	Type of Yarn	Spin	Twist	Ply	Color	Dye
Warp	Cotton	String				White	Natural
Weft	Wool	Commercial	Z	S	4	Red	Aniline
	Wool	Commercial	Z	S	4	White	Natural
	Wool	Commercial	Z	S	4	Purple	Aniline
	Wool	Handspun	Z		1	Black	Aniline

The Twentieth Century

Early Rug Period (1900–20)

The vividly colored eyedazzlers were not very popular with whites as they tended to overpower late Victorian rooms that were already "busy" with a multitude of knickknacks. In an effort to keep the weaving craft alive some traders introduced visual ideas that would appeal to this market. When Americans thought of rugs in the late nineteenth century, they thought of oriental rugs, especially those from the Caucasus region of Russia. Therefore, a number of oriental rug motifs were introduced into Navajo weaving-central medallions, bi-lobed medallions, hooks, "T" shaped elements, and multiple borders (usually two or three each with a different design). This oriental influence is still apparent today, especially in Ganado, Two Gray Hills, and Tees Nos Pos rugs.

Since the late nineteenth century a number of white traders and patrons have been working with individual weavers to create a fine, distinctive and marketable product. Certain styles and colors are associated with trading posts which serve as collecting points for weaving. It is of interest that the most important centers of Navajo rug weaving are close to a source of outside influence, such as a trading post, a railroad, a military outpost, or a town and that they are primarily in the southern and eastern parts of the reservation.

Lorenzo Hubbell was one of the earliest and most famous of the traders to the Navajo. He bought the post at Ganado, Arizona (then called Pueblo Colorado), in 1878 and later went into partnership with C. N. Cotton. Cotton felt that the bright aniline dyes would make their rugs more salable, but Hubbell disagreed and eventually his views won out resulting in a return to more traditional patterns with an emphasis on the old blanket colors of red, white, blue, and black (see no. 76). Weaving quality improved also, as did the patterns and colors. The artist, E. A. Burbank, made small paintings of the best rugs to show to other weavers. These paintings still hang in the post, now a National Monument, and customers can still have copies made to order.

A little later, John B. Moore, in business at Crystal, New Mexico, from the 1890s until 1912, initiated an ambitious program to improve the weaving in his district. Moore limited the use of bright colors, insisting upon natural white, brown, gray, and black with touches of red. He sent Navajo wool to an eastern factory to be scoured and carded by machine. Wool treated in this manner took the dye better and was easier to spin than that processed with the limited amount of water available on the reservation. In 1903 and 1911 Moore published mail-order catalogs for the convenience of distant customers who could order any pattern illustrated in their choice of size and quality of weave. Numbers 79 and 80 are directly out of that 1911 catalog. Moore's illustrated catalogs provide an inventory of patterns that were popular in the first two decades of this century. These patterns, with their many oriental rug motifs, offer quite a contrast to those preferred by Hubbell at Ganado and had a great deal of influence on later weaving styles especially that developed at the post of Two Gray Hills.

76

Blanket
63.34.116

Date: ca. 1900
Gift of Mr. and Mrs. Gilbert Maxwell

Lorenzo Hubbell revival pattern from Ganado, Arizona. Purchased by Clark Field in 1931 from the Irving S. Cobb Collection.

Size: 254 cm. x 144 cm.
Count: 10 warps, 54 wefts.
Selvage: three cords; 4-ply purple aniline dyed commercial yarn.

	Fiber	Type of Yarn	Spin	Twist	Ply	Color	Dye
Warp	Wool	Commercial	Z	S	4	White	Natural
Weft	Wool	Commercial	Z	S	4	White	Natural
	Wool	Commercial	Z	S	4	Black	Aniline
	Wool	Commercial	Z	S	4	Purple	Aniline
	Wool	Commercial	Z	S	4	Red	Aniline

77

Rug
63.34.100

Date: 1915

Gift of Mr. and Mrs. Gilbert Maxwell

Bought in 1915 at Crystal Trading Post by an unknown collector.

Size: 216 cm. x 132 cm.
Count: 7 warps, 24 wefts.
Selvage: two cords; 2-ply aniline dyed red handspun.

	Fiber	Type of Yarn	Spin	Twist	Ply	Color	Dye
Warp	Wool	Handspun	Z		1	White	Natural
Weft	Wool	Handspun	Z		1	White	Natural
	Wool	Handspun	Z		1	Black	Aniline
	Wool	Handspun	Z		1	Gray	Carded
	Wool	Handspun	Z		1	Red	Aniline
	Wool	Handspun	Z		1	Rust	Aniline

See plate section.

78

Rug
63.34.102

Date: 1910–15

Gift of Mr. and Mrs. Gilbert Maxwell

Crystal, see Moore 1911:Plate XXVII.

Size: 222 cm. x 132.5 cm.
Count: 6 warps, 36 wefts.
Selvage: two cords; 3-ply carded gray handspun.

	Fiber	Type of Yarn	Spin	Twist	Ply	Color	Dye
Warp	Wool	Handspun	Z		1	White	Natural
Weft	Wool	Handspun	Z		1	White	Natural
	Wool	Handspun	Z		1	Black	Aniline
	Wool	Handspun	Z		1	Gray	Carded
	Wool	Handspun	Z		1	Med. brown	Aniline

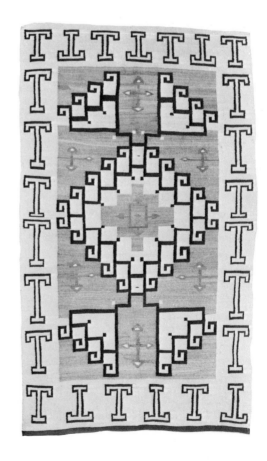

79

Rug
63.34.105

Date: 1910–15
Gift of Mr. and Mrs. Gilbert Maxwell

Bought in 1915 at Crystal Trading Post by an unknown collector. See Moore 1911:Plate XIX; Maxwell 1962:36, fig. 24.

Size: 203.5 cm. x 137.5 cm.
Count: 7 warps, 18 wefts.
Selvage: two cords; 2-ply natural white handspun.

	Fiber	Type of Yarn	Spin	Twist	Ply	Color	Dye
Warp	Wool	Handspun	Z		1	White	Natural
Weft	Wool	Handspun	Z		1	White	Natural
	Wool	Handspun	Z		1	Black	Aniline
	Wool	Handspun	Z		1	Gray	Carded
	Wool	Handspun	Z		1	Red	Aniline
	Wool	Handspun	Z		1	Camel	Aniline (?)

80

Rug
67.67.1

Date: 1900–15
Gift of Mr. George Meyers

Crystal, J. B. Moore influence. The border is a type illustrated in Moore's catalog; the central design is similar to one shown in Moore 1902:Plate V.

Size: 192 cm. x 150 cm.
Count: 7 warps, 18 wefts.
Selvage: two cords; 2-ply white handspun.

	Fiber	Type of Yarn	Spin	Twist	Ply	Color	Dye
Warp	Wool	Handspun	Z	S	3	White	Natural
Weft	Wool	Handspun	Z		1	White	Natural
	Wool	Handspun	Z		1	Black	Aniline
	Wool	Handspun	Z		1	Gray	Carded
	Wool	Handspun	Z		1	Red	Aniline

81

Rug
57.6.3

Date: 1900–15
Gift of Mrs. Willis S. Clayton, Jr.

Size: 176 cm. x 112.5 cm.
Count: 5 warps, 26 wefts.
Selvage: two cords; 3-ply natural white handspun.

	Fiber	Type of Yarn	Spin	Twist	Ply	Color	Dye
Warp	Wool	Handspun	Z		1	White	Natural
Weft	Wool	Handspun	Z		1	White	Natural
	Wool	Handspun	Z		1	Dark brown	Natural
	Wool	Handspun	Z		1	Beige	Carded
	Wool	Handspun	Z		1	Red	Aniline
	Wool	Handspun	Z		1	Maroon	Aniline

82

Rug
63.34.110

Date: ca. 1900
Gift of Mr. and Mrs. Gilbert Maxwell

The material may be the experimental carpet yarn introduced by Lorenzo Hubbell. Note the similarity to no. 83.

Size: 208 cm. x 170 cm.
Count: 8 warps, 40 wefts.
Selvage: two cords; each three strands of 3-ply aniline dyed mottled brown commercial yarn not twisted together but parallel.

See plate section.

	Fiber	Type of Yarn	Spin	Twist	Ply	Color	Dye
Warp	Wool	Commercial	Z	S	3	White	Natural
Weft	Wool	Commercial	Z	S	3	White	Natural
	Wool	Commercial	Z	S	3	Red	Aniline
	Wool	Commercial	Z	S	3	Black	Aniline
	Wool	Commercial	Z	S	3	Mottled brown/ Black	Aniline

Note: In most of the border and in scattered areas in the center the weaver has used the yarn in pairs giving a coarser effect.

83

Rug
74.37.1

Date: 1900–10
Gift of Mrs. Lewis Kohlhaas

Note the similarity of design to no. 82.

Size: 277 cm. x 219 cm.
Count: 5 warps, 20 wefts.
Selvage: two cords; 2-ply handspun aniline dyed red.

	Fiber	Type of Yarn	Spin	Twist	Ply	Color	Dye
Warp	Wool	Handspun	Z		1	White	Natural
Weft	Wool	Handspun	Z		1	White	Natural
	Wool	Handspun	Z		1	Black	Natural+
	Wool	Handspun	Z		1	Gray	Carded
	Wool	Handspun	Z		1	Red	Aniline

Note: Goat hair carded in.

84

Hall Rug
57.6.5

Date: 1900–10
Gift of Mrs. Willis S. Clayton, Jr.

Size: 447 cm. x 92 cm.
Count: 9 warps, 22 wefts.
Selvage: two cords; 2-ply red aniline dyed handspun.

	Fiber	Type of Yarn	Spin	Twist	Ply	Color	Dye
Warp	Cotton	String				White	Natural
Weft	Wool	Handspun	Z		1	White	Natural
	Wool	Handspun	Z		1	Black	Natural+
	Wool	Handspun	Z		1	Gray	Carded
	Wool	Handspun	Z		1	Red	Aniline
	Wool	Handspun	Z		1	Orange	Aniline

85

Saddle Blanket
74.67.1

Date: 1900–20
Gift of Mr. and Mrs. Gilbert Maxwell

Bought in Tucson in 1948.
Size: 129 cm. x 67 cm.
Count: 13 warps, 28 wefts.
Selvage: three cords; 2-ply, each ply a strand of 4-ply white
      commercial yarn.

	Fiber	Type of Yarn	Spin	Twist	Ply	Color	Dye
Warp	Cotton	String				White	Natural
Weft	Wool	Handspun	Z		1	White	Natural
	Wool	Handspun	Z		1	Dark brown	Natural+
	Wool	Handspun	Z		1	Beige	Carded

86

Saddle Blanket
68.16.4

Date: 1900–20
Gift of Miss Elizabeth Elder

A knotted fringe tied to warps at one end.

Size: 69 cm. x 90 cm.
Count: 4 warps, 18 wefts.
Selvage: two cords; 2-ply natural white handspun.

	Fiber	Type of Yarn	Spin	Twist	Ply	Color	Dye
Warp	Wool	Handspun	Z		1	White	Natural
Weft	Wool	Handspun	Z		1	White	Natural
	Wool	Handspun	Z		1	Brown	Natural+
	Wool	Handspun	Z		1	Red	Aniline

Note: Red appears only in one small line extending in from the selvage for
      about 3½ inches.

87

Rug
65.42.162

Date: 1910–20
Transferred from Zimmerman Library,
University of New Mexico.

Size: 183 cm. x 87.5 cm.

Count: 7 warps, 18 wefts.
Selvage: two cords; 2-ply, one gold vegetal dyed handspun
    and the other aniline dyed pink handspun.

	Fiber	Type of Yarn	Spin	Twist	Ply	Color	Dye
Warp	Wool	Handspun	Z		1	White	Natural
Weft	Wool	Handspun	Z		1	White	Natural
	Wool	Handspun	Z		1	Beige	Carded
	Wool	Handspun	Z		1	Gold	Vegetal (?)

88

Rug
65.42.160

Date: 1900–20
Transferred from Zimmerman Library,
University of New Mexico.

Size: 196 cm. x 142.5 cm.
Count: 8 warps, 18 wefts.
Selvage: two cords; 2-ply natural white handspun.

	Fiber	Type of Yarn	Spin	Twist	Ply	Color	Dye
Warp	Cotton	String				White	Natural
Weft	Wool	Handspun	Z		1	White	Natural
	Wool	Handspun	Z		1	Dark brown	Natural
	Wool	Handspun	Z		1	Black	Aniline
	Wool	Handspun	Z		1	Red	Aniline

Note: Red has run uniformly making white background pink.

89

Rug
67.24.1

Date: 1900–10

Gift of Mr. and Mrs. Fred Goldworthy

Family history states it was made in the Zuni area about 1907.

Size: 188 cm. x 131.5 cm.

Count: 6 warps, 16 wefts.

Selvage: two cords; 2-ply natural white handspun.

	Fiber	Type of Yarn	Spin	Twist	Ply	Color	Dye
Warp	Wool	Handspun	Z		1	White	Natural
Weft	Wool	Handspun	Z		1	White	Natural
	Wool	Handspun	Z		1	Brown	Natural
	Wool	Handspun	Z		1	Beige	Carded
	Wool	Handspun	Z		1	Red	Aniline

90

Saddle Blanket
63.33.4

Date: 1900–25

Gift of Mrs. Lawrence Milne

South Kayenta–Shonto Area.

Size: 80 cm. x 91.5 cm.

Count: 8 warps, 16 wefts.

Selvage: two cords; 2-ply dark brown natural handspun.

	Fiber	Type of Yarn	Spin	Twist	Ply	Color	Dye
Warp	Wool	Handspun	Z		1	White	Natural
Weft	Wool	Handspun	Z		1	Dark brown	Natural
	Wool	Handspun	Z		1	Beige	Carded

Modern Regional Styles

Two Gray Hills

When George Bloomfield bought the post at Toadlena, New Mexico, in about 1910, the quality of the weaving in the area was very poor. Bloomfield took a personal interest in improving the quality of the crafts in his area and he would examine rugs closely, point out any defects to the weaver, and explain how they could be corrected. With Ed Davies at the neighboring post of Two Gray Hills he was instrumental in improving the local product. Some designs from Crystal, located on the other side of the Chuska Mountains, were brought into the Two Gray Hills area and between about 1915 and 1925, the distinctive Two Gray Hills style developed. The weavers in this region generally avoid the use of red and their textiles are usually limited to black, white, gray, and brown. They place great stress on precision of design and the use of finely spun yarns, and often weave a spirit trail or narrow line break in the border of a rug.

91

Rug
76.5.1

Date: 1927–28
Gift of Mr. and Mrs. Frederick Johnson

Two Gray Hills.
Won first prize at the Shiprock Fair in 1928.

Size: 213.5 cm. x 139 cm.
Count: 9 warps, 26 wefts.
Selvage: three cords; 2-ply aniline black dyed handspun.

	Fiber	Type of Yarn	Spin	Twist	Ply	Color	Dye
Warp	Wool	Handspun	Z		1	White	Natural
Weft	Wool	Handspun	Z		1	White	Natural
	Wool	Handspun	Z		1	Black	Aniline
	Wool	Handspun	Z		1	Gray	Carded
	Wool	Handspun	Z		1	Camel	Vegetal

92

Rug
76.6.1

Date: 1925–26
Gift of Mr. Julian Shapero

Two Gray Hills.
Purchased in 1927 from George Bloomfield of Toadlena, N.M.
Rug won first prize at the Gallup Ceremonial in 1926.

Size: 183 cm. x 120 cm.
Count: 8 warps, 36 wefts.
Selvage: three cords; 2-ply carded gray handspun.

	Fiber	Type of Yarn	Spin	Twist	Ply	Color	Dye
Warp	Wool	Handspun	Z		1	White	Natural
Weft	Wool	Handspun	Z		1	White	Natural
	Wool	Handspun	Z		1	Black	Aniline (?)
	Wool	Handspun	Z		1	Gray	Carded
	Wool	Handspun	Z		1	Red	Aniline

93

Rug
73.8.1

Date: 1945
Gift of Mr. and Mrs. Gilbert Maxwell

Two Gray Hills.
See Maxwell 1963:26, fig. 12.
Bessie Many Goats, weaver.

Size: 190 cm. x 153.5 cm.
Count: 12 warps, 64 wefts.
Selvage: two cords; 2-ply black aniline (?) dyed handspun.

	Fiber	Type of Yarn	Spin	Twist	Ply	Color	Dye
Warp	Wool	Handspun	Z		1	White	Natural
Weft	Wool	Handspun	Z		1	White	Natural
	Wool	Handspun	Z		1	Black	Aniline (?)
	Wool	Handspun	Z		1	Gray	Carded
	Wool	Handspun	Z		1	Med. brown	Natural
	Wool	Handspun	Z		1	Beige	Natural

Note: Goat hair carded in.

94

Rug
70.24.1

Date: 1960–65
Purchase
Two Gray Hills.

Size: 157 cm. x 84.5 cm.
Count: 12 warps, 38 wefts.
Selvage: two cords; 2-ply carded gray handspun.

	Fiber	Type of Yarn	Spin	Twist	Ply	Color	Dye
Warp	Wool	Handspun	Z		1	White	Natural
Weft	Wool	Handspun	Z		1	White	Natural
	Wool	Handspun	Z		1	Black	Aniline
	Wool	Handspun	Z		1	Gray	Carded
	Wool	Handspun	Z		1	Brown	Natural
						(3 shades)	& carded

Note: Goat hair carded in.

95

Rug
63.34.72

Date: 1961–62
Gift of Mr. and Mrs. Gilbert Maxwell
Two Gray Hills (Toadlena).
Rose Mike, weaver.
Won first prize at Gallup Ceremonial in 1962.

Size: 129 cm. x 89.5 cm.
Count: 15 warps, 96 wefts.
Selvage: two cords; 3-ply carded gray handspun.

	Fiber	Type of Yarn	Spin	Twist	Ply	Color	Dye
Warp	Wool	Handspun	Z		1	White	Natural
Weft	Wool	Handspun	Z		1	White	Natural
	Wool	Handspun	Z		1	Black	Aniline (?)
	Wool	Handspun	Z		1	Brown	Natural
	Wool	Handspun	Z		1	Gray	Carded

96

Rug
69.67.38

Date: 1960s
Gift of Mr. and Mrs. Edwin L. Kennedy

Two Gray Hills.
James Sherman, weaver.

Size: 115 cm. x 76 cm.
Count: 13 warps, 38 wefts.
Selvage: two cords; 2-ply carded gray and natural brown hand-
spun.

	Fiber	Type of Yarn	Spin	Twist	Ply	Color	Dye
Warp	Wool	Handspun	Z		1	White	Natural
Weft	Wool	Handspun	Z		1	White	Natural
	Wool	Handspun	Z		1	Black	Aniline (?)
	Wool	Handspun	Z		1	Gray	Carded
	Wool	Handspun	Z		1	Gray/ Brown	Carded
	Wool	Handspun	Z		1	Brown	Aniline

Note: Goat hair carded in. Wefts not beaten down sufficiently and warp
shows in places.

97

Rug
69.67.17

Date: 1960s
Gift of Mr. and Mrs. Edwin L. Kennedy

Two Gray Hills.
Cora Curley, weaver.

Size: 185.5 cm. x 119.5 cm.
Count: 14 warps, 70 wefts.
Selvage: two cords; 2-ply aniline black dyed handspun.

	Fiber	Type of Yarn	Spin	Twist	Ply	Color	Dye
Warp	Wool	Handspun	Z		1	White	Natural
Weft	Wool	Handspun	Z		1	White	Natural
	Wool	Handspun	Z		1	Black	Aniline (?)
	Wool	Handspun	Z		1	Gray	Carded
	Wool	Handspun	Z		1	Brown	Aniline (?)

Ganado and Klagetoh

The Ganado area continued to carry on the high craft standards set by Lorenzo Hubbell at the beginning of the century. However, the blanket patterns promoted by Hubbell around 1900 have been replaced by oriental type designs with complex borders and a large central pattern. There is no evidence at present to document exactly when this change occurred, but it may have happened around 1915 to 1920 as a result of the success of J. B. Moore's Crystal rugs. Along with the change of pattern went the elimination of the use of blue. The dominance of the colors black, white, gray, and red characterize modern weaving from the Ganado area.

Rugs from Klagetoh have a great stylistic similarity to those from Ganado but frequently include a ribbon motif in the border.

98

Rug
76.40.1
Date: 1920–40
Gift of Mrs. N. W. Shiarella
Ganado.

Size: 259 cm. x 194 cm.
Count: 8 warps, 26 wefts.
Selvage: two cords; 2-ply aniline dyed black handspun.

	Fiber	Type of Yarn	Spin	Twist	Ply	Color	Dye
Warp	Wool	Handspun	Z		1	White	Natural
Weft	Wool	Handspun	Z		1	White	Natural
	Wool	Handspun	Z		1	Red	Aniline
	Wool	Handspun	Z		1	Black	Aniline
	Wool	Handspun	Z		1	Med. brown	Aniline
	Wool	Handspun	Z		1	Gray	Carded

99

Rug
64.84.2

Date: 1920–40
Gift of Mr. Read Mullan

Klagetoh.
Esther Billie, weaver.

Size: 198 cm. x 126 cm.
Count: 7 warps, 30 wefts.
Selvage: two cords; 2-ply aniline dyed black handspun.

	Fiber	Type of Yarn	Spin	Twist	Ply	Color	Dye
Warp	Wool	Handspun	Z		1	White	Natural
Weft	Wool	Handspun	Z		1	White	Natural
	Wool	Handspun	Z		1	Black	Aniline
	Wool	Handspun	Z		1	Beige	Carded & natural
	Wool	Handspun	Z		1	Red	Aniline

100

Rug
73.9.55

Date: 1951
Gift of Mr. and Mrs. Gilbert Maxwell

Ganado.
See Maxwell 1963:38, fig. 28.

Size: 141 cm. x 75 cm.
Count: 10 warps, 32 wefts.
Selvage: no cord, over one warp.

	Fiber	Type of Yarn	Spin	Twist	Ply	Color	Dye
Warp	Wool	Handspun	Z		1	White	Natural
Weft	Wool	Handspun	Z		1	White	Natural
	Wool	Handspun	Z		1	Black	Aniline
	Wool	Handspun	Z		1	Beige	Carded
	Wool	Handspun	Z		1	Red	Aniline

101

Rug
63.47.1

Date: ca. 1930
Gift of Mr. Tobe Turpin

Ganado (?)
This rug was placed in the doorway of the New Mexico exhibit at the Century of Progress Exhibit in Chicago, 1933.

Size: 157 cm. x 90 cm.
Count: 7 warps, 18 wefts.
Selvage: no cord, over one thick brown handspun warp.

	Fiber	Type of Yarn	Spin	Twist	Ply	Color	Dye
Warp	Wool	Handspun	Z		1	White	Natural
Weft	Wool	Handspun	Z		1	White	Natural
	Wool	Handspun	Z		1	Dark brown	Natural+
	Wool	Handspun	Z		1	Beige	Carded
	Wool	Handspun	Z		1	Red	Aniline

102

Rug
63.34.106

Date: ca. 1950
Gift of Mr. and Mrs. Gilbert Maxwell

Ganado.

Size: 153.5 cm. x 107 cm.
Count: 10 warps, 26 wefts.
Selvage: two cords; 2-ply aniline dyed red handspun.

	Fiber	Type of Yarn	Spin	Twist	Ply	Color	Dye
Warp	Wool	Handspun	Z		1	White	Natural
Weft	Wool	Handspun	Z		1	White	Natural
	Wool	Handspun	Z		1	Black	Aniline
	Wool	Handspun	Z		1	Gray	Carded
	Wool	Handspun	Z		1	Red	Aniline

103

Rug
69.67.23

Date: 1960s
Gift of Mr. and Mrs. Edwin L. Kennedy

Ganado.

Size: 197 cm. x 180.5 cm.
Count: 10 warps, 26 wefts.
Selvage: two cords; 2-ply natural brown handspun.

	Fiber	Type of Yarn	Spin	Twist	Ply	Color	Dye
Warp	Wool	Handspun	Z		1	White	Natural
Weft	Wool	Handspun	Z		1	White	Natural
	Wool	Handspun	Z		1	Black	Aniline
	Wool	Commercial	Z	S	4	Red	Aniline
	Wool	Commercial	Z	S	4	Purple	Aniline
	Wool	Commercial	Z	S	4	Gray	Aniline

104

Rug
69.67.22

Date: 1960s
Gift of Mr. and Mrs. Edwin L. Kennedy

Ganado.
Mary Begay, weaver.

Size: 381 cm. x 275 cm.
Count: 7 warps, 44 wefts.
Selvage: two cords; 2-ply aniline dyed medium brown hand-
   spun.

See plate section.

	Fiber	Type of Yarn	Spin	Twist	Ply	Color	Dye
Warp	Wool	Handspun	Z		1	White	Natural
Weft	Wool	Handspun	Z		1	White	Natural
	Wool	Handspun	Z		1	Black	Aniline
	Wool	Handspun	Z		1	Red	Aniline
	Wool	Handspun	Z		1	Beige	Carded

Tees Nos Pos and Red Mesa

Tees Nos Pos in the Four Corners area is the center of a very complex weaving style. The trading post there was built in 1905 by Hambleton Bridger Noel who found that rugs woven by the local Navajo women were of high quality—perhaps due to the influence of a Mrs. Wilson, presumably a missionary in the area around 1890.

Tees Nos Pos rugs frequently have a wide border containing a series of large T's. The central portion is usually filled with a complex design similar to the terraced rectangle that occurs on many modern Ganado rugs. Feathers and arrows are commonly incorporated into the pattern as are many other small elements. Because a wide variety of colors are used, commercial yarns and aniline-dyed handspun wool are the typical yarns used in this area.

Red Mesa is near Tees Nos Pos. Rugs made there are done in what is called the outline style in which every design element (usually a zigzag or a series of them) is outlined in a contrasting color. This is one of the few survivals of the old eyedazzler patterns of the last century, but few rugs are produced in this style now.

105

Rug
63.34.108

Date: ca. 1950
Gift of Mr. and Mrs. Gilbert Maxwell
Tees Nos Pos.
See Maxwell 1963:24, fig. 10.

Size: 184 cm. x 102.5 cm.
Count: 9 warps, 26 wefts.
Selvage: no cord, over two warps twisted together, 4-ply aniline dyed pink commercial yarn.

	Fiber	Type of Yarn	Spin	Twist	Ply	Color	Dye
Warp	Wool	Handspun	Z		1	White	Natural
Weft	Wool	Handspun	Z		1	White	Natural
	Wool	Handspun	Z		1	Black	Aniline
	Wool	Handspun	Z		1	Gray	Carded
	Wool	Handspun	Z		1	Brown	Aniline
	Wool	Handspun	Z		1	Green	Aniline
	Wool	Handspun	Z		1	Purple	Aniline
	Wool	Handspun	Z		1	Turquoise	Aniline
	Wool	Commercial	Z	S	4	Orange	Aniline
	Wool	Commercial	Z	S	4	Blue	Aniline

106

Rug
64.84.1

Date: ca. 1961–62
Gift of Mr. Read Mullan

Tees Nos Pos.
Mrs. Charles Huskay, weaver.
Won second prize at Gallup Ceremonial in 1962.

Size: 291.5 cm. x 194.5 cm.
Count: 10 warps, 26 wefts.
Selvage: two cords; pink and turquoise aniline dyed commercial yarn, one 2-ply and three 4-ply strands twisted together.

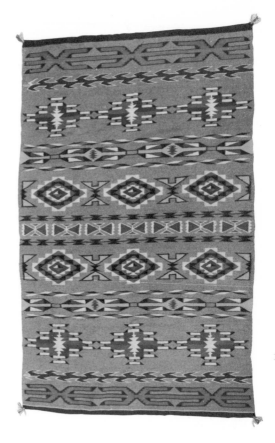

	Fiber	Type of Yarn	Spin	Twist	Ply	Color	Dye
Warp	Wool	Handspun	Z		1	White	Natural
Weft	Wool	Handspun	Z		1	White	Natural
	Wool	Handspun	Z		1	Black	Aniline
	Wool	Handspun	Z		1	Gray	Carded
	Wool	Handspun	Z		1	Cocoa brown	Aniline
	Wool	Handspun	Z		1	Red	Aniline
	Wool	Handspun	Z		1	Purple	Aniline
	Wool	Handspun	Z		1	Turquoise	Aniline
	Wool	Handspun	Z		1	Gold/ Brown	Aniline
	Wool	Handspun	Z		1	Beige	Carded

107

Rug
69.67.27

Date: 1960s
Gift of Mr. and Mrs. Edwin L. Kennedy

Tees Nos Pos.
Sally Begay, weaver.

Size: 273 cm. x 173 cm.
Count: 10 warps, 44 wefts.
Selvage: no cord, over two warps twisted together.

See plate section.

	Fiber	Type of Yarn	Spin	Twist	Ply	Color	Dye
Warp	Wool	Commercial	Z	S	4	Red	Aniline
	Wool	Commercial	Z	S	4	Blue	Aniline
Weft	Wool	Handspun	Z		1	White	Natural
	Wool	Handspun	Z		1	Black	Aniline
	Wool	Handspun	Z		1	Gray	Carded
	Wool	Handspun	Z		1	Beige	Carded
	Wool	Commercial	Z	S	4	Gold/ Brown	Aniline
	Wool	Commercial	Z	S	4	Cocoa	Aniline
	Wool	Commercial	Z	S	4	Pink/ Brown	Aniline
	Wool	Commercial	Z	S	4	Purple	Aniline
	Wool	Commercial	Z	S	4	Red	Aniline
	Wool	Commercial	Z	S	4	Green	Aniline
	Wool	Commercial	Z	S	4	Blue	Aniline
	Wool	Commercial	Z	S	4	Beige	Aniline
	Wool	Commercial	Z	S	4	Gold	Aniline

See plate section.

108

Rug
69.67.26

Date: 1960s
Gift of Mr. and Mrs. Edwin L. Kennedy
Tees Nos Pos.

Size: 300 cm. x 95 cm.
Count: 12 warps, 44 wefts (handspun) and 10 warps, 52 wefts (commercial).
Selvage: three cords; 2-ply black.

	Fiber	Type of Yarn	Spin	Twist	Ply	Color	Dye
Warp	Wool	Handspun	Z		1	White	Natural
Weft	Wool	Handspun	Z		1	White	Natural
	Wool	Handspun	Z		1	Black	Aniline
	Wool	Handspun	Z		1	Gray (dark)	Carded
	Wool	Handspun	Z		1	Gray (light)	Carded
	Wool	Commercial	Z	S	4	Turquoise	Aniline
	Wool	Commercial	Z	S	4	Light brown	Aniline
	Wool	Commercial	Z	S	4	Cocoa	Aniline
	Wool	Commercial	Z	S	4	Mahogany	Aniline
	Wool	Commercial	Z	S	4	Maroon	Aniline
	Wool	Commercial	Z	S	4	Purple	Aniline
	Wool	Commercial	Z	S	4	Green	Aniline

109

Rug
63.34.143

Date: 1900–10
Gift of Mr. and Mrs. Gilbert Maxwell
Red Mesa.
Bought by V. Olsen of Farmington in 1910. See Maxwell 1963: 36, fig. 23.
This rug documents a beginning date for the development of the outline style.

Size: 247 cm. x 145 cm.
Count: 6 warps, 24 wefts.
Selvage: completely redone.

	Fiber	Type of Yarn	Spin	Twist	Ply	Color	Dye
Warp	Wool	Handspun	Z		1	White	Natural
Weft	Wool	Handspun	Z		1	White	Natural
	Wool	Handspun	Z		1	Black	Aniline
	Wool	Handspun	Z		1	Gray	Carded
	Wool	Handspun	Z		1	Yellow	Aniline
	Wool	Handspun	Z		1	Red	Aniline
	Wool	Handspun	Z		1	Green	Aniline
	Wool	Handspun	Z		1	Purple	Aniline
	Wool	Handspun	Z		1	Orange	Aniline
	Wool	Handspun	Z		1	Rust	Aniline

110

Rug
63.33.1

Date: 1920–40
Gift of Mrs. Lawrence Milne

Red Mesa.

Size: 147 cm. x 108 cm.
Count: 5 warps, 22 wefts.
Selvage: two cords; 2-ply aniline dyed red handspun.

	Fiber	Type of Yarn	Spin	Twist	Ply	Color	Dye
Warp	Wool	Handspun	Z		1	White	Natural
Weft	Wool	Handspun	Z		1	White	Natural
	Wool	Handspun	Z		1	Black	Aniline
	Wool	Handspun	Z		1	Gray	Carded
	Wool	Handspun	Z		1	Red	Aniline
	Wool	Handspun	Z		1	Green	Aniline
	Wool	Handspun	Z		1	Pink	Aniline
	Wool	Handspun	Z		1	Rust	Aniline

111

Rug
74.30.2

Date: 1920–30
Gift of Mrs. Dan Falvey

Red Mesa.

Size: 232 cm. x 143 cm.
Count: 10 warps, 30 wefts.
Selvage: two cords; 3-ply natural white handspun.

	Fiber	Type of Yarn	Spin	Twist	Ply	Color	Dye
Warp	Wool	Handspun	Z		1	White	Natural
Weft	Wool	Handspun	Z		1	White	Natural
	Wool	Handspun	Z		1	Black	Aniline
	Wool	Handspun	Z		1	Red	Aniline
	Wool	Handspun	Z		1	Green	Aniline
	Wool	Handspun	Z		1	Orange	Aniline
	Wool	Handspun	Z		1	Purple	Aniline

Vegetal Areas

A revival of old blanket patterns and use of native dyes began in 1920 at Cozy McSparron's trading post at Chinle, Arizona. The movement was initiated by Mary Cabot Wheelwright of Boston, an enthusiastic patron of Native American art who had an Indian crafts shop in Boston and later founded the Museum of Navajo Ceremonial Art in Santa Fe. Miss Wheelwright objected to the use of aniline dyes and foreign designs and wanted the Navajo to dye their own wool with local plants and return to their own classic design traditions. In contrast, the approach at other posts had been to combine Oriental rug patterns with the use of natural sheep colors and touches of aniline red.

Miss Wheelwright financed the project by purchasing all of the weavers' first revival pieces. She secured color pictures of fine old blankets in eastern museums for Mr. McSparron to use as models and the weavers began to produce borderless textiles with horizontal bands of pattern. Several women still remembered some of the old dye formulae and, as the project grew, many weavers experimented with new plants and dye techniques, producing a wide range of pastel colors. Although the new style rugs were enthusiastically received in Boston by Miss Wheelwright's customers, they were resisted by the Gallup wholesalers accustomed to more brightly colored textiles with borders and large central vertically oriented motifs.

Vegetal-dyed rugs are now produced near many trading posts—Crystal, Pine Springs, Wide Ruins, and Burnt Water, as well as in the Chinle district. A distinctive style has developed in each of these regions but vegetal-dyed rugs can be produced anywhere on the reservation. While their patterns are generally like those of blankets produced by the Navajo for their own wear in the nineteenth century, their coloration and heavy dependence on pastel shades give them a quite different visual character. When native dyes appeared at all in early weaving they were used in limited areas often in a thin strip or band.

112

Rug
69.4.3

Date: 1930s
Gift of Mr. Edward C. Groesbeck

Made near the mouth of Canyon de Chelly (Chinle).
The documentation on the date and provenience of this rug indicate that not all weavers in this area adopted the new vegetal style.

Size: 193 cm. x 112.5 cm.
Count: 6 warps, 20 wefts.
Selvage: two cords; 2-ply dark brown natural handspun.

	Fiber	Type of Yarn	Spin	Twist	Ply	Color	Dye
Warp	Wool	Handspun	Z		1	White	Natural
	Wool	Handspun	Z		1	Beige	Carded
Weft	Wool	Handspun	Z		1	White	Natural
	Wool	Handspun	Z		1	Dark brown	Natural
	Wool	Handspun	Z		1	Beige	Carded
	Wool	Handspun	Z		1	Red	Aniline

113

Rug
63.33.2

Date: 1930s
Gift of Mrs. Lawrence Milne

Size: 143.5 cm. x 99 cm.
Count: 6 warps, 18 wefts.
Selvage: two cords; 2-ply carded beige handspun.

	Fiber	Type of Yarn	Spin	Twist	Ply	Color	Dye
Warp	Wool	Handspun	Z		1	White	Natural
Weft	Wool	Handspun	Z		1	White	Natural
	Wool	Handspun	Z		1	Brown	Natural
	Wool	Handspun	Z		1	Beige	Carded
	Wool	Handspun	Z		1	Red	Aniline
	Wool	Handspun	Z		1	Maroon	Aniline
	Wool	Handspun	Z		1	Pink	Carded
	Wool	Handspun	Z		1	Yellow	Aniline

114

Rug

63.34.175

Date: ca. 1935

Gift of Mr. and Mrs. Gilbert Maxwell

Chinle.

Size: 242 cm. x 166 cm.

Count: 9 warps, 28 wefts.

Selvage: two cords; 2-ply carded gray handspun.

	Fiber	Type of Yarn	Spin	Twist	Ply	Color	Dye
Warp	Wool	Handspun	Z		1	White	Natural
Weft	Wool	Handspun	Z		1	White	Natural
	Wool	Handspun	Z		1	Dark brown	Dupont
	Wool	Handspun	Z		1	Gold	Dupont
	Wool	Handspun	Z		1	Light gold	Dupont
	Wool	Handspun	Z		1	Orange	Aniline (?)
	Wool	Handspun	Z		1	Purple	Aniline (?)

Note: The chemical dyes used in this rug were experimental and designed to simulate the soft colors of Navajo vegetal or native dyes with more readily available synthetics. The experiment was short-lived.

115

Rug

65.47.3

Date: 1930–34

Gift of Dr. W. W. Hill

Bought by Dr. Hill at Chinle in 1934.

Size: 119 cm. x 95 cm.

Count: 10 warps, 24 wefts.

Selvage: two cords; 2-ply aniline dyed purple handspun.

	Fiber	Type of Yarn	Spin	Twist	Ply	Color	Dye
Warp	Wool	Handspun	Z		1	White	Natural
Weft	Wool	Handspun	Z		1	White	Natural
	Wool	Handspun	Z		1	Brown	Natural
	Wool	Handspun	Z		1	Yellow	Vegetal

116

Rug
65.47.4

Date: 1934
Gift of Dr. W. W. Hill

Chinle.

Size: 135 cm. x 84 cm.
Count: 7 warps, 22 wefts.
Selvage: two cords; 2-ply vegetal dyed gold handspun.

	Fiber	Type of Yarn	Spin	Twist	Ply	Color	Dye
Warp	Wool	Handspun	Z		1	White	Natural
Weft	Wool	Handspun	Z		1	White	Natural
	Wool	Handspun	Z		1	Green/Gold	Vegetal

117

Rug
65.47.7

Date: ca. 1934
Gift of Dr. W. W. Hill

Chinle.

Size: 127.5 cm. x 66 cm.
Count: 10 warps, 26 wefts.
Selvage: two cords; 2-ply natural brown handspun.

	Fiber	Type of Yarn	Spin	Twist	Ply	Color	Dye
Warp	Wool	Handspun	Z		1	White	Natural
Weft	Wool	Handspun	Z		1	White	Natural
	Wool	Handspun	Z		1	Black	Natural+
	Wool	Handspun	Z		1	Gray	Carded
	Wool	Handspun	Z		1	Gold	Vegetal
	Wool	Handspun	Z		1	Med. brown	Vegetal

118

Rug
65.57.14

Date: 1920–40
Gift of Mr. Raymond Jonson,
Vera Jonson Memorial Collection

Probably Chinle or Crystal.

See plate section.

Size: 229 cm. x 140 cm.
Count: 7 warps, 18 wefts.
Selvage: two cords; 2-ply natural white handspun.

	Fiber	Type of Yarn	Spin	Twist	Ply	Color	Dye
Warp	Wool	Handspun	Z		1	White	Natural
Weft	Wool	Handspun	Z		1	White	Natural
	Wool	Handspun	Z		1	Brown	Natural
	Wool	Handspun	Z		1	Gold (2 shades)	Vegetal
	Wool	Handspun	Z		1	Green/ Beige	Vegetal

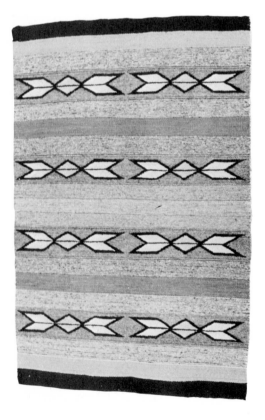

119

Rug
73.9.57

Date: 1954
Gift of Mr. and Mrs. Gilbert Maxwell

Crystal.

Size: 127 cm. x 86 cm.
Count: 8 warps, 26 wefts.
Selvage: three cords; 3-ply natural white handspun.

	Fiber	Type of Yarn	Spin	Twist	Ply	Color	Dye
Warp	Wool	Handspun	Z		1	White	Natural
Weft	Wool	Handspun	Z		1	White	Natural
	Wool	Handspun	Z		1	Black	Natural+
	Wool	Handspun	Z		1	Gray	Carded
	Wool	Handspun	Z		1	Gold	Vegetal
	Wool	Handspun	Z		1	Rust	Vegetal
	Wool	Handspun	Z		1	Light green	Vegetal

120

Rug
63.34.86

Date: 1944
Gift of Mr. and Mrs. Gilbert Maxwell

Fort Wingate School.

Mr. Maxwell notes that these experimental dyes were expensive and this rug was one of only seventy-five made with chrome dyes.

Size: 157.5 cm. x 104.5 cm.
Count: 8 warps, 44 wefts.
Selvage: three cords; 2-ply handspun (one blue, one pink, one beige) chrome dyed.

	Fiber	Type of Yarn	Spin	Twist	Ply	Color	Dye
Warp	Wool	Handspun	Z			Gray	Carded
Weft	Wool	Handspun	Z		1	White	Chrome
	Wool	Handspun	Z		1	Brown	Chrome
	Wool	Handspun	Z		1	Pink	Chrome
	Wool	Handspun	Z		1	Peach	Chrome
	Wool	Handspun	Z		1	Light blue	Chrome
	Wool	Handspun	Z		1	Med. blue	Chrome
	Wool	Handspun	Z		1	Russet	Chrome

See plate section.

121

Rug
69.67.36

Date: 1960s
Gift of Mr. and Mrs. Edwin L. Kennedy

Wide Ruins.
Annie Apache, weaver.

Size: 132 cm. x 85 cm.
Count: 8 warps, 40 wefts.
Selvage: two cords; 2-ply natural white handspun.

	Fiber	Type of Yarn	Spin	Twist	Ply	Color	Dye
Warp	Wool	Handspun	Z		1	White	Natural
Weft	Wool	Handspun	Z		1	White	Natural
	Wool	Handspun	Z		1	Gray	Vegetal
	Wool	Handspun	Z		1	Gold	Vegetal
	Wool	Handspun	Z		1	Med. brown	Natural

122

Rug
69.67.35

Date: 1960s
Gift of Mr. and Mrs. Edwin L. Kennedy
Wide Ruins (?)
Emma K. Joe, weaver.

Size: 127 cm. x 76 cm.
Count: 9 warps, 28 wefts.
Selvage: two cords; 1-ply vegetal dyed gray handspun.

	Fiber	Type of Yarn	Spin	Twist	Ply	Color	Dye
Warp	Wool	Handspun	Z		1	White	Natural
Weft	Wool	Handspun	Z		1	White	Natural
	Wool	Handspun	Z		1	Gray	Vegetal
	Wool	Handspun	Z		1	Gold	Vegetal
	Wool	Handspun	Z		1	Beige	Vegetal

123

Rug
69.67.44

Date: 1960s
Gift of Mr. and Mrs. Edwin L. Kennedy
Possibly Wide Ruins or Chinle.

Size: 92 cm. x 55 cm.
Count: 8 warps, 48 wefts.
Selvage: two cords; 2-ply natural white handspun.

	Fiber	Type of Yarn	Spin	Twist	Ply	Color	Dye
Warp	Cotton	String				White	Natural
Weft	Wool	Handspun	Z		1	White	Natural
	Wool	Commercial	Z	S	4	Black	Aniline
	Wool	Commercial	Z	S	4	Brown	Aniline
	Wool	Commercial	Z	S	4	Red	Aniline
	Wool	Commercial	Z	S	4	Purple	Aniline
	Wool	Commercial	Z	S	4	Yellow	Aniline
	Wool	Commercial	Z	S	4	Orange	Aniline
	Wool	Commercial	Z	S	4	Turquoise	Aniline
	Wool	Commercial	Z	S	4	Med. blue	Aniline
	Wool	Commercial	Z	S	4	Pink	Aniline

124

Rug
63.34.146

Date: 1953
Gift of Mr. and Mrs. Gilbert Maxwell

Nazlini.
Mary Van Winkle, weaver.

Size: 217 cm. x 125 cm.
Count: 10 warps, 26 wefts.
Selvage: two cords; 2-ply natural white handspun.

	Fiber	Type of Yarn	Spin	Twist	Ply	Color	Dye
Warp	Wool	Handspun	Z		1	White	Natural
Weft	Wool	Handspun	Z		1	White	Natural
	Wool	Handspun	Z		1	Black	Aniline
	Wool	Handspun	Z		1	Gray	Carded
	Wool	Handspun	Z		1	Yellow	Aniline (?)
	Wool	Handspun	Z		1	Brown	Natural
	Wool	Handspun	Z		1	Red	Aniline
	Wool	Handspun	Z		1	Green	Aniline

125

Rug
63.34.127a

Date: 1960–61
Gift of Mr. and Mrs. Gilbert Maxwell

Pine Springs.
Ellen Smith, weaver.
Won special award at Gallup Ceremonial in 1961.

Size: 109 cm. x 56.5 cm.
Count: 10 warps, 44 wefts.
Selvage: three cords; 2-ply vegetal dyed beige handspun.

	Fiber	Type of Yarn	Spin	Twist	Ply	Color	Dye
Warp	Wool	Handspun	Z		1	White	Natural
Weft	Wool	Handspun	Z		1	White	Natural
	Wool	Handspun	Z		1	Gray	Vegetal
	Wool	Handspun	Z		1	Gold	Vegetal
	Wool	Handspun	Z		1	Green/Gold	Vegetal
	Wool	Handspun	Z		1	Lt. brown	Vegetal
	Wool	Handspun	Z		1	Yellow	Vegetal
	Wool	Handspun	Z		1	Peach	Vegetal

126

Rug
63.34.127b

Date: 1960–61
Gift of Mr. and Mrs. Gilbert Maxwell

Pine Springs.
Angie Smith (age 14), weaver, granddaughter of Ellen Smith who wove 63.34.127a. Won second prize in the juvenile division at the Gallup Ceremonial in 1961.

Size: 108.5 cm. x 55 cm.
Count: 10 warps, 44 wefts.
Selvage: three cords; 2-ply vegetal dyed beige handspun.

	Fiber	Type of Yarn	Spin	Twist	Ply	Color	Dye
Warp	Wool	Handspun	Z		1	White	Natural
Weft	Wool	Handspun	Z		1	White	Natural
	Wool	Handspun	Z		1	Gold	Vegetal
	Wool	Handspun	Z		1	Gray	Vegetal
	Wool	Handspun	Z		1	Green/Gold	Vegetal
	Wool	Handspun	Z		1	Light brown	Vegetal
	Wool	Handspun	Z		1	Yellow	Vegetal
	Wool	Handspun	Z		1	Peach	Vegetal

127

Rug
69.67.25

Date: 1960s
Gift of Mr. and Mrs. Edwin L. Kennedy

Size: 285 cm. x 185 cm.
Count: 8 warps, 36 wefts.
Selvage: three cords; 2-ply vegetal dyed gray handspun.

	Fiber	Type of Yarn	Spin	Twist	Ply	Color	Dye
Warp	Wool	Handspun	Z		1	White	Natural
Weft	Wool	Handspun	Z		1	White	Natural
	Wool	Handspun	Z		1	Gray	Carded
	Wool	Handspun	Z		1	Gray	Vegetal
	Wool	Handspun	Z		1	Gold	Vegetal
	Wool	Handspun	Z		1	Pink	Vegetal
	Wool	Handspun	Z		1	Rust	Vegetal

Four Corners

Most of the Museum's weaving from this area is illustrated in the Sandpainting Design and Twill sections. The two specimens here, both pillow backs or throws, are of a generalized style notable for the use of bright colors similar to those of the sandpainting textiles from this area.

128

Rug
69.67.46

Date: 1960s
Gift of Mr. and Mrs. Edwin L. Kennedy

Four Corners Area.

Size: 99 cm. x 63 cm.
Count: 8 warps, 40 wefts.
Selvage: two cords; 3-ply natural white handspun.

	Fiber	Type of Yarn	Spin	Twist	Ply	Color	Dye
Warp	Cotton	String				White	Natural
Weft	Wool	Commercial	Z	S	4	White	Natural
	Wool	Commercial	Z	S	4	Black	Aniline
	Wool	Commercial	Z	S	4	Gray	Aniline
	Wool	Commercial	Z	S	4	Cocoa	Aniline
	Wool	Commercial	Z	S	4	Purple	Aniline
	Wool	Commercial	Z	S	4	Red	Aniline
	Wool	Commercial	Z	S	4	Orange	Aniline
	Wool	Commercial	Z	S	4	Turquoise	Aniline

129

Pillow Top
69.67.41

Date: 1960s
Gift of Mr. and Mr. Edwin L. Kennedy

Four Corners Area.

Size: 55 cm. x 46 cm.
Count: 8 warps, 28 wefts.
Selvage: no cord, over two warps.

	Fiber	Type of Yarn	Spin	Twist	Ply	Color	Dye
Warp	Wool	Handspun	Z		1	White	Natural
Weft	Wool	Handspun	Z		1	White	Natural
	Wool	Handspun	Z		1	Black	Aniline
	Wool	Handspun	Z		1	Gray	Carded
	Wool	Handspun	Z		1	Beige	Carded
	Wool	Handspun	Z		1	Yellow/Brown	Aniline

Unknown Provenience (1920–present)

Many twentieth-century Navajo textiles are of a pattern that cannot readily be attributed to any particular weaving area. They may have originated near one of the previously mentioned trading posts such as Ganado or Two Gray Hills but lack the characteristics of these styles. Most may be from locales where traders did not encourage manufacture of an identifiable local product.

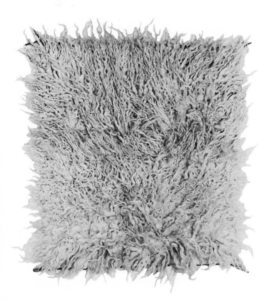

130

Rug
63.13.2

Date: 1930s
Gift of Mr. Tom Bahti

Tapestry weave with tufts of goat hair woven in about 1 inch apart. This type of textile is frequently placed in front of a loom and used by the weaver as a mat or cushion.

Size: 72.5 cm. x 66 cm.
Count: 6 warps, 18 wefts.
Selvage: no cord, over two warps twisted together.

	Fiber	Type of Yarn	Spin	Twist	Ply	Color	Dye
Warp	Wool	Handspun	Z		1	Black	Aniline
	Wool	Handspun	Z		1	Turquoise	Aniline
	Wool	Handspun	Z		1	Purple	Aniline
	Wool	Handspun	Z		1	White	Natural
Weft	Wool	Handspun	Z		1	White	Natural

131

Saddle Blanket
74.28.3

Date: 1920–40
Donor unknown

Size: 59 cm. x 64 cm.
Count: 8 warps, 40 wefts.
Selvage: completely missing.

	Fiber	Type of Yarn	Spin	Twist	Ply	Color	Dye
Warp	Wool	Handspun	Z		1	White	Natural
Weft	Wool	Handspun	Z		1	White	Natural
	Wool	Handspun	Z		1	Brown	Natural+
	Wool	Handspun	Z		1	Beige	Carded
	Wool	Handspun	Z		1	Red	Aniline

132

Rug
66.113.1

Date: 1920–40
Gift of Mrs. Prudence E. Oakes

Size: 167 cm. x 118 cm.
Count: 7 warps, 24 wefts.
Selvage: two cords; 3-ply aniline dyed blue handspun.

	Fiber	Type of Yarn	Spin	Twist	Ply	Color	Dye
Warp	Wool	Handspun	Z		1	Brown	Natural
Weft	Wool	Handspun	Z		1	Red	Aniline
	Wool	Handspun	Z		1	White	Natural
	Wool	Handspun	Z		1	Yellow	Aniline
	Wool	Handspun	Z		1	Purple	Aniline

133

Rug
65.47.5

Date: ca. 1930
Gift of Dr. W. W. Hill

Bought at Mesa Verde, Colorado.

Size: 123.5 cm. x 80 cm.
Count: 8 warps, 36 wefts.
Selvage: two cords; 3-ply natural dark brown handspun.

	Fiber	Type of Yarn	Spin	Twist	Ply	Color	Dye
Warp	Wool	Handspun	Z		1	White	Natural
Weft	Wool	Handspun	Z		1	White	Natural
	Wool	Handspun	Z		1	Dark brown	Natural+
	Wool	Handspun	Z		1	Med. brown	Natural
	Wool	Handspun	Z		1	Beige	Carded
	Wool	Handspun	Z		1	Camel	Vegetal (?)

134

Rug
65.47.6

Date: ca. 1930
Gift of Dr. W. W. Hill
Bought at Mesa Verde, Colorado.

Size: 92.5 cm. x 44.5 cm.
Count: 8 warps, 26 wefts.
Selvage: two cords; 2-ply carded beige handspun.

	Fiber	Type of Yarn	Spin	Twist	Ply	Color	Dye
Warp	Wool	Handspun	Z		1	White	Natural
Weft	Wool	Handspun	Z		1	White	Natural
	Wool	Handspun	Z		1	Dark brown	Natural+
	Wool	Handspun	Z		1	Beige	Carded

135

Rug
74.28.4

Date: 1920–40
Donor unknown

Possibly Chinle.

Size: 200 cm. x 118 cm.
Count: 6 warps, 16 wefts.
Selvage: two cords; 3-ply natural brown handspun.

	Fiber	Type of Yarn	Spin	Twist	Ply	Color	Dye
Warp	Wool	Handspun	Z		1	White	Natural
Weft	Wool	Handspun	Z		1	White	Natural
	Wool	Handspun	Z		1	Brown	Natural
	Wool	Handspun	Z		1	Beige	Carded

136

Rug
66.113.4

Date: 1920–40
Gift of Mrs. Prudence E. Oakes

Size: 190 cm. x 144 cm.
Count: 5 warps, 24 wefts.
Selvage: two cords; 2-ply natural white handspun.

	Fiber	Type of Yarn	Spin	Twist	Ply	Color	Dye
Warp	Wool	Handspun	Z		1	White	Natural
Weft	Wool	Handspun	Z		1	White	Natural
	Wool	Handspun	Z		1	Black	Natural+
	Wool	Handspun	Z		1	Brown	Natural
	Wool	Handspun	Z		1	Red	Aniline
	Wool	Handspun	Z		1	Beige	Carded

Note: The red color is sometimes termed "Ganado red."

137

Rug
72.49.58

Date: 1930s
Gift of Mr. and Mrs. Gilbert Maxwell

Size: 162 cm. x 91 cm.
Count: 6 warps, 26 wefts.
Selvage: two cords; 3-ply aniline dyed gray handspun.

	Fiber	Type of Yarn	Spin	Twist	Ply	Color	Dye
Warp	Wool	Handspun	Z		1	White	Natural
Weft	Wool	Handspun	Z		1	White	Natural
	Wool	Handspun	Z		1	Black	Aniline
	Wool	Handspun	Z		1	Gray	Aniline
	Wool	Handspun	Z		1	Red	Aniline
	Wool	Handspun	Z		1	Orange	Aniline
	Wool	Handspun	Z		1	Yellow	Aniline
	Wool	Handspun	Z		1	Green	Aniline
	Wool	Handspun	Z		1	Maroon	Aniline

138

Saddle Blanket
61.1.10

Date: 1950–60
Gift of Mr. Tom Bahti

Double weave and shaped.

Size: 70 cm. x 88 cm.
Count: 5 warps, 18 wefts.

Selvage: three cords; 2-ply natural white handspun goat hair.

	Fiber	Type of Yarn	Spin	Twist	Ply	Color	Dye
Warp	Wool	Handspun	Z		1	White	Natural
Weft	Wool	Handspun	Z		1	White	Natural
	Wool	Handspun	Z		1	Black	Aniline
	Wool	Handspun	Z		1	Red	Aniline
	Wool	Handspun	Z		1	Orange/Brown	Aniline

139

Rug
63.34.152

Date: ca. 1946
Gift of Mr. and Mrs. Gilbert Maxwell

Double weave.
See Maxwell 1963:41, fig. 33.

Size: 147 cm. x 105 cm.
Count: 6 warps, 28 wefts.
Selvage: three cords; 2-ply aniline dyed red handspun.

	Fiber	Type of Yarn	Spin	Twist	Ply	Color	Dye
Warp	Cotton	String				White	Natural
Weft	Wool	Handspun	Z		1	White	Natural
	Wool	Handspun	Z		1	Black	Aniline
	Wool	Handspun	Z		1	Gray/Beige	Carded
	Wool	Handspun	Z		1	Red	Aniline
	Wool	Handspun	Z		1	Orange/Brown	Aniline

140

Rug
63.33.3

Date: 1920–40
Gift of Mrs. Lawrence Milne

Size: 128 cm. x 75 cm.
Count: 7 warps, 20 wefts.
Selvage: two cords; 2-ply natural brown handspun on one side,
　　　　single ply natural brown handspun on the other.

	Fiber	Type of Yarn	Spin	Twist	Ply	Color	Dye
Warp	Wool	Handspun	Z		1	White	Natural
Weft	Wool	Handspun	Z		1	Dark brown	Natural+
	Wool	Handspun	Z		1	Med. brown	Natural
	Wool	Handspun	Z		1	Beige	Carded
	Wool	Handspun	Z		1	Red	Aniline

Twills

The twill weave was a popular Pueblo technique which the Navajo used for one-piece dresses and saddle blankets in the late nineteenth century. Types of twill vary from plain, diagonal, and herringbone to more complicated diamond patterns which the Navajo call "many eyes" (see: nos. 146–48). Most twentieth-century twills are double saddle blankets which are now made in larger sizes for use as rugs.

141

Blanket
63.34.183

Date: 1880–90
Gift of Mr. and Mrs. Gilbert Maxwell

Purchased from Carlsbad Caverns Supply Co. in 1946. Registered with Laboratory of Anthropology, Santa Fe, no. 626. Twill weave.

Size: 141.5 cm. x 87 cm.
Selvage: two cords; 3-ply aniline dyed red handspun. The cords are tied into small tassels 43 cm. from one end.

	Fiber	Type of Yarn	Spin	Twist	Ply	Color	Dye
Warp	Wool	Handspun	Z		1	White	Natural
Weft	Wool	Handspun	Z		1	Red	Aniline
	Wool	Handspun	Z		1	Orange	Aniline
	Wool	Handspun	Z		1	Green	Aniline
	Wool	Handspun	Z		1	Blue	Indigo
	Wool	Handspun	Z		1	White	Natural

142

Saddle Blanket
63.34.181

Date: 1880–1900
Gift of Mr. and Mrs. Gilbert Maxwell

Purchased in 1946 from Carlsbad Caverns Supply Co. Registered with the Laboratory of Anthropology, Santa Fe, no. 645. Diagonal twill weave.

Size: 102 cm. x 75.5 cm.
Selvage: two cords; 2-ply aniline dyed red handspun.

	Fiber	Type of Yarn	Spin	Twist	Ply	Color	Dye
Warp	Wool	Handspun	Z		1	White	Natural
Weft	Wool	Handspun	Z		1	White	Natural
	Wool	Handspun	Z		1	Black	Natural+
	Wool	Handspun	Z		1	Orange	Aniline
	Wool	Handspun	Z		1	Green	Aniline
	Wool	Handspun	Z		1	Red	Aniline

143

Saddle Blanket
63.33.5

Date: 1895–1910
Gift of Mrs. Lawrence Milne

Plain twill weave.

Size: 126 cm. x 77 cm.
Selvage: two cords; 2-ply orange aniline dyed handspun.

	Fiber	Type of Yarn	Spin	Twist	Ply	Color	Dye
Warp	Wool	Handspun	Z		1	White	Natural
Weft	Wool	Handspun	Z		1	White	Natural
	Wool	Handspun	Z		1	Red	Aniline
	Wool	Handspun	Z		1	Blue	Indigo
	Wool	Handspun	Z		1	Green	Indigo & yellow
	Wool	Handspun	Z		1	Pink	Carded

144

Saddle Blanket
74.37.2

Date: 1900–20
Gift of Mrs. Lewis Kohlhaas

Twill weave.

Size: 131 cm. x 85.5 cm.
Selvage: three cords; 2-ply aniline dyed handspun, one red, one yellow.

	Fiber	Type of Yarn	Spin	Twist	Ply	Color	Dye
Warp	Wool	Handspun	Z		1	White	Natural
Weft	Wool	Handspun	Z		1	White	Natural
	Wool	Handspun	Z		1	Black	Natural+
	Wool	Handspun	Z		1	Gray	Carded
	Wool	Handspun	Z		1	Red	Aniline

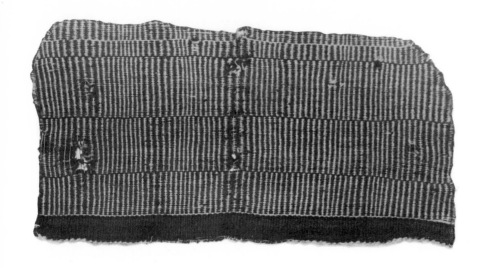

145

Saddle Blanket Fragment
55.20.43

Date: 1880–1900
Gift of Mrs. Richard Wetherill
Plain twill weave.

Size: 42 cm. x 85 cm.
Selvage: completely missing.

	Fiber	Type of Yarn	Spin	Twist	Ply	Color	Dye
Warp	Wool	Handspun	Z		1	Pink	White with aniline red run onto it
Weft	Wool	Handspun	Z		1	Brown	Natural
	Wool	Handspun	Z		1	Red	Aniline

146

Saddle Blanket
60.27.124

Date: ca. 1930
Gift of Betty Karlson Lane,
Muriel Karlson Memorial Collection

Twill weave.

Size: 124 cm. x 74 cm.
Selvage: no cord, over one warp.

	Fiber	Type of Yarn	Spin	Twist	Ply	Color	Dye
Warp	Wool	Handspun	Z		1	Brown	Natural
Weft	Wool	Handspun	Z		1	Dark brown	Natural
	Wool	Handspun	Z		1	White	Natural
	Wool	Handspun	Z		1	Beige	Carded
	Wool	Handspun	Z		1	Red	Aniline
	Wool	Handspun	Z		1	Orange	Aniline
	Wool	Handspun	Z		1	Rust/ Brown	Carded orange

147

Saddle Blanket
63.34.95

Date: ca. 1960
Gift of Mr. and Mrs. Gilbert Maxwell

Gallup.
Diamond twill weave.

Size: 141.5 cm. x 85.5 cm.
Selvage: three cords; 3-ply aniline dyed black handspun.

	Fiber	Type of Yarn	Spin	Twist	Ply	Color	Dye
Warp	Wool	Handspun	Z		1	White	Natural
Weft	Wool	Handspun	Z		1	White	Natural
	Wool	Handspun	Z		1	Black	Aniline
	Wool	Handspun	Z		1	Gray	Carded

148

Saddle Blanket
63.34.96

Date: ca. 1948
Gift of Mr. and Mrs. Gilbert Maxwell

Wide Ruins.
See Maxwell 1963:49, fig. 38.
Plain and diamond twill weave.

Size: 152.5 cm. x 86 cm.
Selvage: two cords; 2-ply vegetal dyed beige handspun.

	Fiber	Type of Yarn	Spin	Twist	Ply	Color	Dye
Warp	Wool	Handspun	Z		1	Gray	Carded
Weft	Wool	Handspun	Z		1	White	Natural
	Wool	Handspun	Z		1	Beige	Vegetal
	Wool	Handspun	Z		1	Gray	Carded

149

Saddle Blanket
63.34.92

Date: ca. 1960
Gift of Mr. and Mrs. Gilbert Maxwell
Gallup.
Diamond twill weave.

Size: 139.5 cm. x 86.5 cm.
Selvage: three cords; 2-ply aniline dyed gray handspun.

	Fiber	Type of Yarn	Spin	Twist	Ply	Color	Dye
Warp	Wool	Handspun	Z		1	White	Natural
Weft	Wool	Handspun	Z		1	White	Natural
	Wool	Handspun	Z		1	Black	Aniline
	Wool	Handspun	Z		1	Med. brown	Aniline

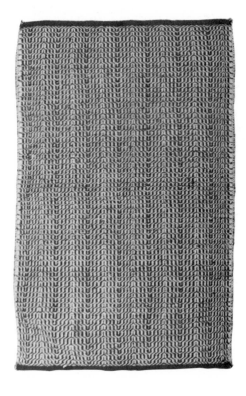

150

Saddle Blanket
63.34.93

Date: ca. 1960
Gift of Mr. and Mr. Gilbert Maxwell
Gallup.
Plain twill weave.

Size: 138 cm. x 87.5 cm.
Selvage: two cords; 2-ply natural white handspun.

	Fiber	Type of Yarn	Spin	Twist	Ply	Color	Dye
Warp	Cotton	String				White	Natural
Weft	Wool	Handspun	Z		1	White	Natural
	Wool	Handspun	Z		1	Black	Aniline
	Wool	Handspun	Z		1	Orange	Aniline

151

Saddle Blanket
63.34.94

Date: ca. 1952
Gift of Mr. and Mrs. Gilbert Maxwell

Gallup.
See Maxwell 1963:46, fig. 37.
Twill weave.

Size: 147 cm. x 82 cm.
Selvage: three cords; 3-ply aniline dyed handspun, two brown
and one maroon.

	Fiber	Type of Yarn	Spin	Twist	Ply	Color	Dye
Warp	Wool	Handspun	Z		1	White	Natural
Weft	Wool	Handspun	Z		1	White	Natural
	Wool	Handspun	Z		1	Black	Aniline
	Wool	Handspun	Z		1	Gray	Carded

152

Saddle Blanket
63.34.90

Date: ca. 1960
Gift of Mr. and Mrs. Gilbert Maxwell

Gallup.
Diamond twill weave.

Size: 137 cm. x 94.5 cm.
Selvage: three cords; one 2-ply black, one 2-ply red, one 2-ply
white handspun.

	Fiber	Type of Yarn	Spin	Twist	Ply	Color	Dye
Warp	Wool	Handspun	Z		1	White	Natural
Weft	Wool	Handspun	Z		1	White	Natural
	Wool	Handspun	Z		1	Black	Aniline
	Wool	Handspun	Z		1	Red	Aniline

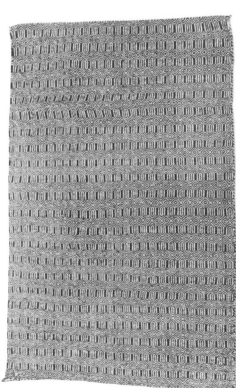

Pictorials

Although pictorial elements were used in blankets as early as the 1860s, the earliest extant pictorial rugs date from the 1890s. Weavers often used representations as design patterns, altering the forms of natural objects or reversing the letters of a word to make them better suited to the composition of the rug.

153

Rug
63.40.3

Date: 1910–40
Gift of Mr. George A. Johnston

Size: 159 cm. x 104.5 cm.
Count: 8 warps, 32 wefts.
Selvage: missing; some fragments indicate 2-ply red aniline handspun.

	Fiber	Type of Yarn	Spin	Twist	Ply	Color	Dye
Warp	Wool	Handspun	Z		1	White	Natural
	Wool	Handspun	Z		1	Dark brown	Natural
Weft	Wool	Handspun	Z		1	White	Natural
	Wool	Handspun	Z		1	Dark brown	Natural+
	Wool	Handspun	Z		1	Med. brown	Natural
	Wool	Handspun	Z		1	Beige	Carded
	Wool	Handspun	Z		1	Red	Aniline

154

Kilt
67.126.3

Date: ca. 1950
Gift of Mr. and Mrs. Gilbert Maxwell

Made by a Navajo weaver as a copy of or substitute for a Pueblo embroidered kilt.

Size: 70 cm. x 93 cm.
Count: 10 warps, 52 wefts.
Selvage: three cords; 2-ply, each 4-ply aniline red dyed commercial yarn.

	Fiber	Type of Yarn	Spin	Twist	Ply	Color	Dye
Warp	Cotton	String				White	Natural
Weft	Wool	Commercial	Z	S	4	White	Natural
	Wool	Commercial	Z	S	4	Black	Aniline
	Wool	Commercial	Z	S	4	Red	Aniline
	Wool	Commercial	Z	S	4	Orange	Aniline
	Wool	Commercial	Z	S	4	Purple	Aniline
	Wool	Commercial	Z	S	4	Turquoise	Aniline
	Wool	Commercial	Z	S	4	Green	Aniline

77. Navajo rug

82. Navajo rug

104. Navajo rug

107. Navajo rug

109. Navajo rug

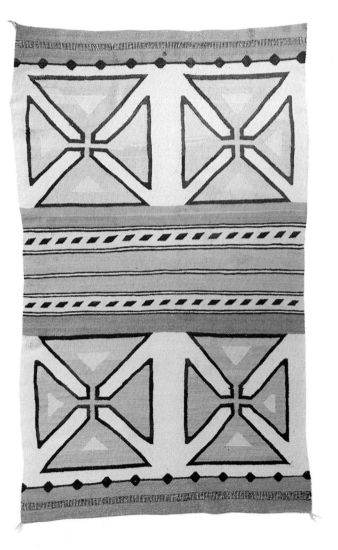

118. Navajo rug

120. Navajo rug

163. Navajo rug, Yei

155

Blanket
63.34.115

Date: 1948
Gift of Mr. and Mrs. Gilbert Maxwell

Lukachukai.
Mary Woodman, weaver.
A copy of a Pendleton Mills machine-woven woman's shawl with a knotted maroon wool fringe on all four sides. There are no lazy lines in the piece to imitate the machine-made cloth.

Size: 147 cm. x 145.5 cm.
Count: 13 warps, 6 wefts.
Selvage: no cord, over two twisted warps (natural brown hand-spun).

	Fiber	Type of Yarn	Spin	Twist	Ply	Color	Dye
Warp	Wool	Handspun	Z		1	White	Natural
Weft	Wool	Handspun	Z		1	Med. brown	Natural
	Wool	Handspun	Z		1	Dark brown	Aniline
	Wool	Handspun	Z		1	Red	Aniline
	Wool	Handspun	Z		1	Maroon	Aniline
	Wool	Handspun	Z		1	Yellow	Aniline
	Wool	Handspun	Z		1	Orange	Aniline
	Wool	Handspun	Z		1	Turquoise	Aniline
	Wool	Handspun	Z		1	Rust	Aniline
	Wool	Commercial	Z	S	4	White	Natural

156

Rug
74.65.1

Date: 1920–40
Purchase by Greater UNM Fund

Size: 125.5 cm. x 92 cm.
Count: 10 warps, 24 wefts.
Selvage: two cords; 2-ply aniline dyed dark green handspun.

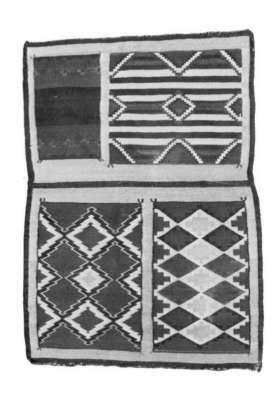

	Fiber	Type of Yarn	Spin	Twist	Ply	Color	Dye
Warp	Wool	Handspun	Z		1	White	Natural
Weft	Wool	Handspun	Z		1	White	Natural
	Wool	Handspun	Z		1	Dark brown	Natural
	Wool	Handspun	Z		1	Gray	Carded
	Wool	Handspun	Z		1	Red	Aniline
	Wool	Handspun	Z		1	Yellow	Aniline
	Wool	Handspun	Z		1	Dark green	Aniline
	Wool	Handspun	Z		1	Purple	Aniline

Note: The red color is sometimes termed "Ganado red."

157

Rug
70.39.41

Date: 1950–60
Gift of Mr. and Mrs. Bruce T. Ellis

Size: 61 cm. x 54.5 cm.
Count: 7 warps, 28 wefts.
Selvage: two cords; 3-ply turquoise aniline dyed handspun.

	Fiber	Type of Yarn	Spin	Twist	Ply	Color	Dye
Warp	Wool	Handspun	Z		1	Brown	Natural
Weft	Wool	Handspun	Z		1	White	Natural
	Wool	Handspun	Z		1	Black	Aniline
	Wool	Handspun	Z		1	Red	Aniline
	Wool	Handspun	Z		1	Gold	Vegetal (?)

158

Rug
69.67.18

Date: 1960s
Gift of Mr. and Mrs. Edwin L. Kennedy

Atsuma Blackhorse, weaver.
Copy of a Pablita Velarde painting.

Size: 137 cm. x 99 cm.
Count: 10 warps, 36 wefts.
Selvage: two cords; 2-ply, each a strand of 4-ply aniline dyed
      maroon commercial yarn.

	Fiber	Type of Yarn	Spin	Twist	Ply	Color	Dye
Warp	Cotton	String				White	Natural
Weft	Wool	Commercial	Z	S	4	White	Natural
	Wool	Commercial	Z	S	4	Black	Aniline
	Wool	Commercial	Z	S	4	Gray	Aniline
	Wool	Commercial	Z	S	4	Maroon	Aniline
	Wool	Commercial	Z	S	4	Purple	Aniline
	Wool	Commercial	Z	S	4	Yellow	Aniline
	Wool	Commercial	Z	S	4	Gold	Aniline
	Wool	Commercial	Z	S	4	Lavender	Aniline
	Wool	Commercial	Z	S	4	Green	Aniline
	Wool	Commercial	Z	S	4	Med. rose	Aniline

159

Rug, Pictorial
63.34.172

Date: 1962
Gift of Mr. and Mrs. Gilbert Maxwell

Lukachukai.
Margaret Bochinclozy, weaver.
See Maxwell 1963:40, fig. 32.

Size: 170 cm. x 124.5 cm.
Count: 7 warps, 30 wefts.
Selvage: no cord, over two warps twisted together.

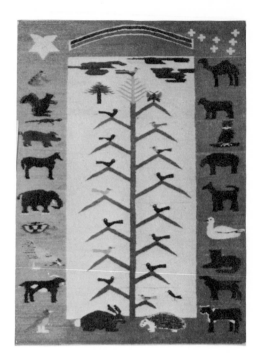

	Fiber	Type of Yarn	Spin	Twist	Ply	Color	Dye
Warp	Wool	Handspun	Z		1	White	Natural
Weft	Wool	Handspun	Z		1	White	Natural
	Wool	Handspun	Z		1	Gray	Carded
	Wool	Handspun	Z		1	Black	Aniline
	Wool	Handspun	Z		1	Brown	Aniline
	Wool	Handspun	Z		1	Red	Aniline
	Wool	Handspun	Z		1	Gold	Aniline
	Wool	Handspun	Z		1	Turquoise	Aniline
	Wool	Handspun	Z		1	Bright blue	Aniline
	Wool	Handspun	Z		1	Yellow	Aniline

Sandpainting Design

Since the late nineteenth century the Four Corners area, especially near Farmington, has been a center of manufacture of rugs that utilize Navajo ritual subject matter. These rugs have no function in Navajo ceremonies but are made solely to sell to white collectors. Figures of the Navajo supernaturals called "yeis" were among the earliest ritual subjects represented in weaving. Many Navajos considered these representations to be sacrilegious but the rugs sold, and "ceremonial" weaving has been produced ever since (Amsden 1934:106). A modern variation of this type of rug is the Yeibichai which represents masked dancers from the Night Chant rather than the yeis themselves.

The first sandpainting rug was made in 1896 near Chaco Canyon (Wheat 1975). Sandpainting (or dry paintings) are an integral part of Navajo sings or curing rituals and are executed in colored sands and vegetal materials. They are ephemeral, made to be used and destroyed in the space of one day; however, a number of Navajo medicine men or singers have cooperated with researchers to record the rituals and the paintings associated with them. This cooperation has led to the publication of chantways and reproductions of dry paintings in books. Rugs that reproduce sandpaintings are often based on published illustrations, but some are executed from the weaver's memory of sings she has witnessed.

Weavers always change some detail of the design of a sandpainting rug to avoid the sacrilege of making a holy painting in permanent form. Even so, such work is considered a misuse of power by many Navajos and some weavers will not show sandpainting design rugs to their neighbors but take them directly to the trading post to avoid community disapproval. After successfully completing such a rug a weaver may have a purifying sing before she executes another.

Yei and Yeibichai

160

Rug, Yei
63.34.101
Date: 1910
Gift of Mr. and Mrs. Gilbert Maxwell
Gallegos.
Size: 167 cm. x 97.5 cm.
Count: 9 warps, 30 wefts.
Selvage: two cords; 2-ply gray handspun.

	Fiber	Type of Yarn	Spin	Twist	Ply	Color	Dye
Warp	Cotton	String				White	Natural
Weft	Wool	Handspun	Z		1	White	Natural
	Wool	Handspun	Z		1	Dark gray	Aniline
	Wool	Handspun	Z		1	Gray	Carded
	Wool	Handspun	Z		1	Red	Aniline
	Wool	Handspun	Z		1	Orange	Aniline
	Wool	Commercial	Z	S	4	Turquoise	Aniline

161

Rug, Yei
68.16.3

Date: 1920–40
Gift of Miss Elizabeth Elder

Shiprock-Farmington Area.

Size: 71 cm. x 62 cm.
Count: 10 warps, 40 wefts (handspun) and 10 warps, 48 wefts
      (commercial).
Selvage: no cord, over one warp.

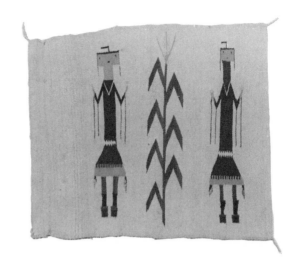

	Fiber	Type of Yarn	Spin	Twist	Ply	Color	Dye
Warp	Cotton	String				White	Natural
Weft	Wool	Handspun	Z		1	White	Natural
	Wool	Handspun	Z		1	Gray	Aniline
	Wool	Commercial	Z	S	4	Brown	Aniline
	Wool	Commercial	Z	S	4	Maroon	Aniline
	Wool	Commercial	Z	S	4	Orange	Aniline
	Wool	Commercial	Z	S	4	Green	Aniline

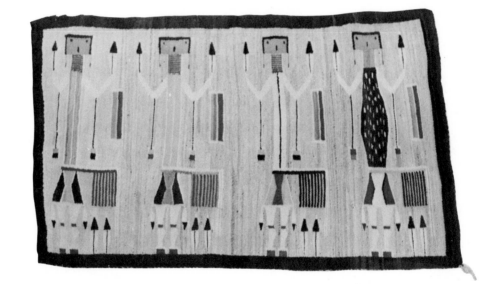

162

Rug, Yei
65.47.9

Date: ca. 1934
Gift of Dr. W. W. Hill

Lukachukai.

Size: 121.5 cm. x 73.5 cm.
Count: 8 warps, 32 wefts.
Selvage: two cords; 2-ply natural white handspun.

	Fiber	Type of Yarn	Spin	Twist	Ply	Color	Dye
Warp	Wool	Handspun	Z		1	White	Natural
Weft	Wool	Handspun	Z		1	White	Natural
	Wool	Handspun	Z		1	Brown	Natural
	Wool	Handspun	Z		1	Camel	Vegetal (?)
	Wool	Handspun	Z		1	Red	Aniline
	Wool	Handspun	Z		1	Orange	Aniline
	Wool	Handspun	Z		1	Purple	Aniline
	Wool	Handspun	Z		1	Gray	Aniline

163

Rug, Yei
69.67.32

Date: 1960s
Gift of Mr. and Mrs. Edwin L. Kennedy
Farmington Area.

Size: 140 cm. x 89.5 cm.
Count: 12 warps, 44 wefts.
Selvage: two cords; 3-ply, each a 4-ply
      strand of aniline dyed black
      commercial yarn.

	Fiber	Type of Yarn	Spin	Twist	Ply	Color	Dye
Warp	Cotton	String				White	Natural
Weft	Wool	Commercial	Z	S	4	White	Natural
	Wool	Commercial	Z	S	4	Black	Aniline
	Wool	Commercial	Z	S	4	Gray	Aniline
	Wool	Commercial	Z	S	4	Red	Aniline
	Wool	Commercial	Z	S	4	Green	Aniline
	Wool	Commercial	Z	S	4	Brown	Aniline

See plate section.

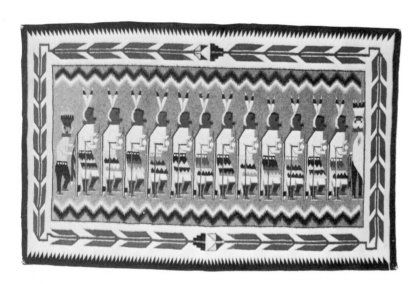

164

Rug, Yeibichai Dance from Nightway
63.34.150

Date: 1960
Gift of Mr. and Mrs. Gilbert Maxwell
Shiprock.

Mrs. Tom Peshlakai, weaver.
Size: 172 cm. x 107.5 cm.
Count: 12 warps, 34 wefts.
Selvage: no cord, over two warps.

	Fiber	Type of Yarn	Spin	Twist	Ply	Color	Dye
Warp	Wool	Handspun	Z		1	White	Natural
Weft	Wool	Commercial	Z	S	4	White	Natural
	Wool	Commercial	Z	S	4	Black	Aniline
	Wool	Commercial	Z	S	4	Gray	Aniline
	Wool	Commercial	Z	S	4	Red	Aniline
	Wool	Commercial	Z	S	4	Orange	Aniline
	Wool	Commercial	Z	S	4	Pink	Aniline
	Wool	Commercial	Z	S	4	Purple	Aniline
	Wool	Commercial	Z	S	4	Med. green	Aniline
	Wool	Commercial	Z	S	4	Forest green	Aniline
	Wool	Commercial	Z	S	4	Magenta	Aniline
	Wool	Commercial	Z	S	4	Yellow	Aniline
	Wool	Commercial	Z	S	4	Gold	Aniline
	Wool	Commercial	Z	S	4	Hot pink	Aniline
	Wool	Commercial	Z	S	4	Light blue	Aniline
	Wool	Commercial	Z	S	4	Turquoise	Aniline
	Wool	Commercial	Z	S	4	Med. brown	Aniline

165

Rug, Adaptation of Yeibichai Dance from Nightway
69.67.28

Date: 1960s
Gift of Mr. and Mrs. Edwin L. Kennedy

Shiprock.

Size: 912 cm. x 144 cm.
Count: 11 warps, 40 wefts.
Selvage: no cord, over one warp.

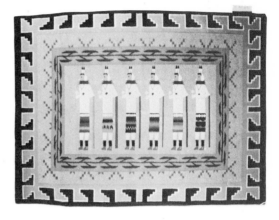

	Fiber	Type of Yarn	Spin	Twist	Ply	Color	Dye
Warp	Wool	Handspun	Z		1	White	Natural
Weft	Wool	Commercial	Z	S	4	White	Natural
	Wool	Commercial	Z	S	4	Black	Aniline
	Wool	Commercial	Z	S	4	Gray	Aniline
	Wool	Commercial	Z	S	4	Cocoa	Aniline
	Wool	Commercial	Z	S	4	Red	Aniline
	Wool	Commercial	Z	S	4	Rose	Aniline
	Wool	Commercial	Z	S	4	Green	Aniline
	Wool	Commercial	Z	S	4	Blue	Aniline
	Wool	Commercial	Z	S	4	Turquoise	Aniline
	Wool	Commercial	Z	S	4	Yellow	Aniline
	Wool	Commercial	Z	S	4	Purple	Aniline

Water Chant

166

Rug, Sandpainting
70.75.1

Date: 1960s
Gift of Mr. and Mrs. Edwin L. Kennedy

The Water Chant.
Red Rock.
This rug and the following three make a complete set of copies
of the sandpaintings of the Water Chant as published in Wheel-
wright 1946:195–201.
Alberta Thomas, weaver.

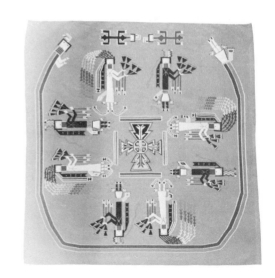

Size: 157.5 cm. x 156 cm.
Count: 14 warps, 54 wefts.
Selvage: no cord, over two warps.

	Fiber	Type of Yarn	Spin	Twist	Ply	Color	Dye
Warp	Wool	Commercial	Z	S	2	White	Natural
Weft	Wool	Commercial	Z	S	2	White	Natural
	Wool	Commercial	Z	S	2	Black	Aniline
	Wool	Commercial	Z	S	2	Med. brown	Aniline
	Wool	Commercial	Z	S	2	Red	Aniline
	Wool	Commercial	Z	S	2	Royal blue	Aniline
	Wool	Commercial	Z	S	2	Turquoise	Aniline
	Wool	Commercial	Z	S	2	Gold	Aniline

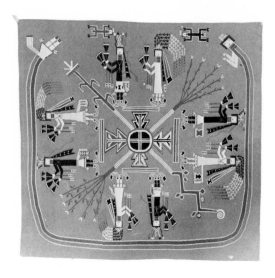

167

Rug, Sandpainting
70.75.2

Date: 1960s
Gift of Mr. and Mrs. Edwin L. Kennedy
The Water Chant.
Red Rock.
Anna May Tanner, weaver.

Size: 164 cm. x 160 cm.
Count: 15 warps, 52 wefts.
Selvage: no cord, over one warp.

	Fiber	Type of Yarn	Spin	Twist	Ply	Color	Dye
Warp	Wool	Handspun	Z		1	White	Natural
Weft	Wool	Commercial	Z	S	2	White	Natural
	Wool	Commercial	Z	S	2	Black	Aniline
	Wool	Commercial	Z	S	2	Red	Aniline
	Wool	Commercial	Z	S	2	Med. brown	Aniline
	Wool	Commercial	Z	S	2	Yellow	Aniline
	Wool	Commercial	Z	S	2	Royal blue	Aniline
	Wool	Commercial	Z	S	2	Turquoise	Aniline

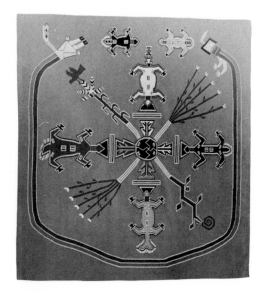

168

Rug, Sandpainting
70.75.3

Date: 1960s
Gift of Mr. and Mrs. Edwin L. Kennedy
The Water Chant.
Red Rock.
Alberta Thomas, weaver.

Size: 141 cm. x 150.5 cm.
Count: 15 warps, 60 wefts.
Selvage: no cord, over one warp.

	Fiber	Type of Yarn	Spin	Twist	Ply	Color	Dye
Warp	Wool	Handspun	Z		1	White	Natural
Weft	Wool	Commercial	Z	S	2	Med. brown	Aniline
	Wool	Commercial	Z	S	2	Black	Aniline
	Wool	Commercial	Z	S	2	White	Natural
	Wool	Commercial	Z	S	2	Red	Aniline
	Wool	Commercial	Z	S	2	Gold	Aniline
	Wool	Commercial	Z	S	2	Royal blue	Aniline

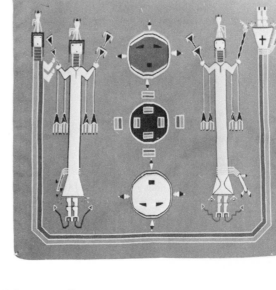

169

Rug, Sandpainting
70.54.4

Date: 1960s
Gift of Mr. and Mrs. Edwin L. Kennedy

The Water Chant.
Red Rock.
Alberta Thomas, weaver.

Size: 133 cm. x 124 cm.
Count: 14 warps, 56 wefts.
Selvage: no cord, over one warp.

	Fiber	Type of Yarn	Spin	Twist	Ply	Color	Dye
Warp	Wool	Commercial	Z	S	2	White	Natural
Weft	Wool	Commercial	Z	S	2	White	Natural
	Wool	Commercial	Z	S	2	Black	Aniline
	Wool	Commercial	Z	S	2	Med. brown	Aniline
	Wool	Commercial	Z	S	2	Royal blue	Aniline
	Wool	Commercial	Z	S	2	Red	Aniline
	Wool	Commercial	Z	S	2	Yellow	Aniline

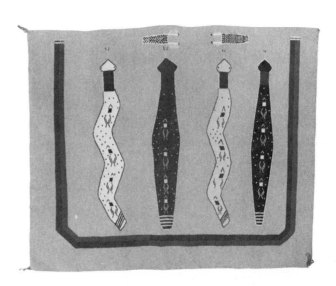

Beautyway

170

Rug, Sandpainting
69.67.1

Date: 1960s
Gift of Mr. and Mrs. Edwin L. Kennedy

Beautyway: Big Snakes.
Red Rock.
This rug and the following fifteen comprise a
complete set of copies of published illustrations
of the Beautyway Sandpaintings and were
commissioned by Mr. Kennedy.
See Wyman 1957:Plate I–XVI.
Mrs. King Tutt, weaver.

Size: 128 cm. x 103 cm.
Count: 13 warps, 52 wefts.
Selvage: no cord, over one warp.

	Fiber	Type of Yarn	Spin	Twist	Ply	Color	Dye
Warp	Wool	Handspun	Z		1	White	Natural
Weft	Wool	Commercial	Z	S	2	Gray	Aniline
	Wool	Commercial	Z	S	2	White	Natural
	Wool	Commercial	Z	S	2	Black	Aniline
	Wool	Commercial	Z	S	2	Yellow	Aniline
	Wool	Commercial	Z	S	2	Red	Aniline
	Wool	Commercial	Z	S	2	Royal blue	Aniline

171

Rug, Sandpainting
69.67.2

Date: 1960s
Gift of Mr. and Mrs. Edwin L. Kennedy

Beautyway: Crooked Big Snakes.
Red Rock.
Mrs. King Tutt, weaver.

Size: 104 cm. x 109 cm.
Count: 10 warps, 40 wefts.
Selvage: no cord, over one warp.

	Fiber	Type of Yarn	Spin	Twist	Ply	Color	Dye
Warp	Wool	Handspun	Z		1	White	Natural
Weft	Wool	Commercial	Z	S	2	Gray	Aniline
	Wool	Commercial	Z	S	2	Black	Aniline
	Wool	Commercial	Z	S	2	White	Natural
	Wool	Commercial	Z	S	2	Royal blue	Aniline
	Wool	Commercial	Z	S	2	Yellow	Aniline
	Wool	Commercial	Z	S	2	Red	Aniline

172

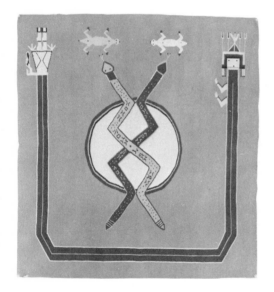

Rug, Sandpainting
69.67.3

Date: 1960s
Gift of Mr. and Mrs. Edwin L. Kennedy

Beautyway: Snakes on Their House.
Red Rock.
Mrs. King Tutt, weaver.

Size: 104 cm. x 107 cm.
Count: 14 warps, 52 wefts.
Selvage: no cord, over one warp.

	Fiber	Type of Yarn	Spin	Twist	Ply	Color	Dye
Warp	Wool	Handspun	Z		1	White	Natural
Weft	Wool	Commercial	Z	S	2	White	Natural
	Wool	Commercial	Z	S	2	Rust/Pink	Aniline
	Wool	Commercial	Z	S	2	Gold	Aniline
	Wool	Commercial	Z	S	2	Royal blue	Aniline
	Wool	Commercial	Z	S	2	Red	Aniline
	Wool	Commercial	Z	S	2	Black	Aniline

173

Rug, Sandpainting
69.67.4

Date: 1960s
Gift of Mr. and Mrs. Edwin L. Kennedy

Beautyway: Sandpainting at Dropped-out Mountain.
Red Rock.
Anna Mae Tanner, weaver.

Size: 111 cm. x 108.5 cm.
Count: 12 warps, 56 wefts.
Selvage: no cord, over one warp.

	Fiber	Type of Yarn	Spin	Twist	Ply	Color	Dye
Warp	Wool	Handspun	Z		1	White	Natural
Weft	Wool	Commercial	Z	S	2	Gold	Aniline
	Wool	Commercial	Z	S	2	White	Natural
	Wool	Commercial	Z	S	2	Black	Aniline
	Wool	Commercial	Z	S	2	Light blue	Aniline
	Wool	Commercial	Z	S	2	Royal blue	Aniline
	Wool	Commercial	Z	S	2	Yellow	Aniline
	Wool	Commercial	Z	S	2	Red	Aniline
	Wool	Commercial	Z	S	2	Turquoise	Aniline

174

Rug, Sandpainting
69.67.5

Date: 1960s
Gift of Mr. and Mrs. Edwin L. Kennedy

Beautyway: Snakes and Clouds.
Red Rock.
Anna Mae Tanner, weaver.
Size: 112.5 cm. x 109.5 cm.
Count: 12 warps, 48 wefts.
Selvage: no cord, over one warp.

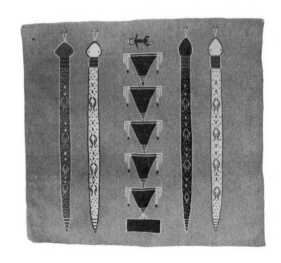

	Fiber	Type of Yarn	Spin	Twist	Ply	Color	Dye
Warp	Wool	Handspun	Z		1	White	Natural
	Wool	Handspun	Z		1	Beige	Vegetal
Weft	Wool	Commercial	Z	S	2	Gray	Aniline
	Wool	Commercial	Z	S	2	White	Natural
	Wool	Commercial	Z	S	2	Black	Aniline
	Wool	Commercial	Z	S	2	Med. blue	Aniline
	Wool	Commercial	Z	S	2	Yellow	Aniline
	Wool	Commercial	Z	S	2	Red	Aniline
	Wool	Commercial	Z	S	2	Turquoise	Aniline

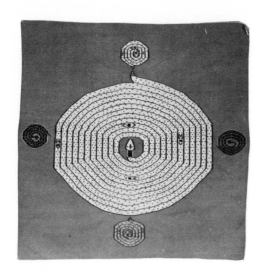

175

Rug, Sandpainting
69.67.6

Date: 1960s
Gift of Mr. and Mrs. Edwin L. Kennedy
Beautyway: Big Snake with No End.
Red Rock.
Mrs. King Tutt, weaver.

Size: 135.5 cm. x 131 cm.
Count: 14 warps, 52 wefts.
Selvage: no cord, over one warp.

	Fiber	Type of Yarn	Spin	Twist	Ply	Color	Dye
Warp	Wool	Handspun	Z		1	White	Natural
Weft	Wool	Commercial	Z	S	2	Mustard yellow	Aniline
	Wool	Commercial	Z	S	2	White	Natural
	Wool	Commercial	Z	S	2	Black	Aniline
	Wool	Commercial	Z	S	2	Royal blue	Aniline
	Wool	Commercial	Z	S	2	Red	Aniline

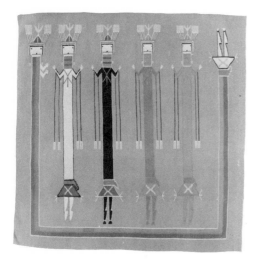

176

Rug, Sandpainting
69.67.7
Date: 1960s
Gift of Mr. and Mrs. Edwin L. Kennedy

Beautyway: Snake Pollen People.
Red Rock.
Lorraine Tallman, weaver.

Size: 115 cm. x 112 cm.
Count: 14 warps, 40 wefts.
Selvage: two cords; 4-ply aniline dyed beige commercial yarn.

	Fiber	Type of Yarn	Spin	Twist	Ply	Color	Dye
Warp	Wool	Handspun	Z		1	White	Natural
Weft	Wool	Commercial	Z	S	2	Beige	Aniline
	Wool	Commercial	Z	S	2	White	Natural
	Wool	Commercial	Z	S	2	Black	Aniline
	Wool	Commercial	Z	S	2	Light blue	Aniline
	Wool	Commercial	Z	S	2	Lavender	Aniline
	Wool	Commercial	Z	S	2	Gold	Aniline
	Wool	Commercial	Z	S	2	Rust	Aniline
	Wool	Commercial	Z	S	2	Pink	Aniline

Note: Rug ends in two inches of twill executed in 4-ply commercial yarn.

177

Rug, Sandpainting
69.67.8

Date: 1960s
Gift of Mr. and Mrs. Edwin L. Kennedy

Beautyway: The Mountain Gods.
Red Rock.
Ruby Denea, weaver.

Size: 151 cm. x 106 cm.
Count: 11 warps, 60 wefts.
Selvage: no cord, over one warp.

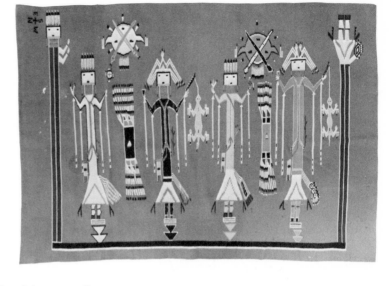

	Fiber	Type of Yarn	Spin	Twist	Ply	Color	Dye
Warp	Wool	Handspun	Z		1	White	Natural
Weft	Wool	Commercial	Z	S	2	Gold	Aniline
	Wool	Commercial	Z	S	2	Yellow	Aniline
	Wool	Commercial	Z	S	2	White	Natural
	Wool	Commercial	Z	S	2	Black	Aniline
	Wool	Commercial	Z	S	2	Red	Aniline
	Wool	Commercial	Z	S	2	Light blue	Aniline
	Wool	Commercial	Z	S	2	Raspberry	Aniline
	Wool	Commercial	Z	S	2	Green	Aniline
	Wool	Commercial	Z	S	2	Royal blue	Aniline

178

Rug, Sandpainting
69.67.9

Date: 1960s
Gift of Mr. and Mrs. Edwin L. Kennedy

Beautyway: People of the Myth.
Red Rock.
Anna Mae Tanner, weaver.

Size: 139 cm. x 148.5 cm.
Count: 13 warps, 60 wefts.
Selvage: no cord, over one warp.

See plate section.

	Fiber	Type of Yarn	Spin	Twist	Ply	Color	Dye
Warp	Wool	Handspun	Z		1	White	Natural
Weft	Wool	Commercial	Z	S	2	Rust/Pink	Aniline
	Wool	Commercial	Z	S	2	Black	Aniline
	Wool	Commercial	Z	S	2	White	Natural
	Wool	Commercial	Z	S	2	Royal blue	Aniline
	Wool	Commercial	Z	S	2	Yellow	Aniline
	Wool	Commercial	Z	S	2	Red	Aniline
	Wool	Commercial	Z	S	2	Turquoise	Aniline

179

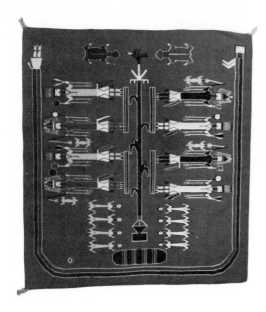

Rug, Sandpainting
69.67.10

Date: 1960s

Gift of Mr. and Mrs. Edwin L. Kennedy

Beautyway: People with Weasel Skins.
Red Rock.
Mrs. King Tutt, weaver.

Size: 164.5 cm. x 156 cm.

Count: 11 warps, 44 wefts.

Selvage: no cord, over one warp.

	Fiber	Type of Yarn	Spin	Twist	Ply	Color	Dye
Warp	Wool	Handspun	Z		1	White	Natural
Weft	Wool	Commercial	Z	S	2	White	Natural
	Wool	Commercial	Z	S	2	Black	Aniline
	Wool	Commercial	Z	S	2	Light brown	Aniline
	Wool	Commercial	Z	S	2	Yellow	Aniline
	Wool	Commercial	Z	S	2	Turquoise	Aniline
	Wool	Commercial	Z	S	2	Red	Aniline
	Wool	Commercial	Z	S	2	Royal blue	Aniline

180

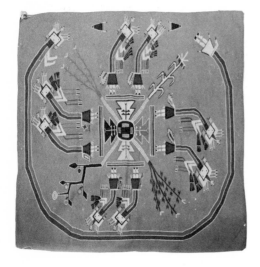

Rug, Sandpainting
69.67.11

Date: 1960s

Gift of Mr. and Mrs. Edwin L. Kennedy

Beautyway: Rainbow People.
Red Rock.
Mrs. King Tutt, weaver.

Size: 166 cm. x 151.5 cm.

Count: 14 warps, 52 wefts.

Selvage: no cord, over one warp.

	Fiber	Type of Yarn	Spin	Twist	Ply	Color	Dye
Warp	Wool	Handspun	Z		1	White	Natural
Weft	Wool	Commercial	Z	S	2	Beige	Aniline
	Wool	Commercial	Z	S	2	Brown	Aniline
	Wool	Commercial	Z	S	2	Black	Aniline
	Wool	Commercial	Z	S	2	White	Natural
	Wool	Commercial	Z	S	2	Red	Aniline
	Wool	Commercial	Z	S	2	Turquoise	Aniline
	Wool	Commercial	Z	S	2	Yellow	Aniline
	Wool	Commercial	Z	S	2	Purple	Aniline
	Wool	Commercial	Z	S	2	Royal blue	Aniline
	Wool	Commercial	Z	S	2	Light blue	Aniline

181

Rug, Sandpainting
69.67.12

Date: 1960s
Gift of Mr. and Mrs. Edwin L. Kennedy

Beautyway: At Moved-out Mountain.
Red Rock.
Mrs. James Etcitty, weaver.

Size: 120 cm. x 121 cm.
Count: 12 warps, 52 wefts.
Selvage: no cord, over one warp.

	Fiber	Type of Yarn	Spin	Twist	Ply	Color	Dye
Warp	Cotton	String				White	Natural
Weft	Wool	Commercial	Z	S	2	Peach	Aniline
	Wool	Commercial	Z	S	2	Black	Aniline
	Wool	Commercial	Z	S	2	White	Natural
	Wool	Commercial	Z	S	2	Red	Aniline
	Wool	Commercial	Z	S	2	Turquoise	Aniline
	Wool	Commercial	Z	S	2	Yellow	Aniline
	Wool	Commercial	Z	S	2	Green	Aniline

See plate section.

182

Rug, Sandpainting
69.67.13

Date: 1961
Gift of Mr. and Mrs. Edwin L. Kennedy

Beautyway: Water Creatures.
Red Rock.
Won first prize at Gallup Ceremonial in 1962.
Anna Mae Tanner, weaver.

Size: 146 cm. x 144 cm.
Count: 14 warps, 60 wefts.
Selvage: no cord, over one warp.

	Fiber	Type of Yarn	Spin	Twist	Ply	Color	Dye
Warp	Wool	Handspun	Z		1	White	Natural
Weft	Wool	Commercial	Z	S	2	Gray	Aniline
	Wool	Commercial	Z	S	2	White	Natural
	Wool	Commercial	Z	S	2	Black	Aniline
	Wool	Commercial	Z	S	2	Royal blue	Aniline
	Wool	Commercial	Z	S	2	Yellow	Aniline
	Wool	Commercial	Z	S	2	Green	Aniline
	Wool	Commercial	Z	S	2	Red	Aniline
	Wool	Commercial	Z	S	2	Turquoise	Aniline
	Wool	Commercial	Z	S	2	Magenta	Aniline

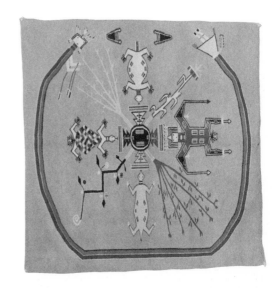

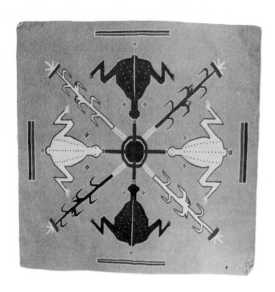

183

Rug, Sandpainting
69.67.14

Date: 1960s
Gift of Mr. and Mrs. Edwin L. Kennedy

Beautyway: Frogs.
Red Rock.
Anna Mae Tanner, weaver.

Size: 133 cm. x 135.5 cm.
Count: 12 warps, 60 wefts.
Selvage: no cord, over one warp.

	Fiber	Type of Yarn	Spin	Twist	Ply	Color	Dye
Warp	Wool	Handspun	Z		1	Beige	Vegetal
Weft	Wool	Commercial	Z	S	2	Gray	Aniline
	Wool	Commercial	Z	S	2	White	Natural
	Wool	Commercial	Z	S	2	Black	Aniline
	Wool	Commercial	Z	S	2	Yellow	Aniline
	Wool	Commercial	Z	S	2	Turquoise	Aniline
	Wool	Commercial	Z	S	2	Red	Aniline
	Wool	Commercial	Z	S	2	Royal blue	Aniline

184

Rug, Sandpainting
69.67.15

Date: 1960s
Gift of Mr. and Mrs. Edwin L. Kennedy

Beautyway: Big Thunder.
Red Rock.
Mrs. King Tutt, weaver.

Size: 135 cm. x 122 cm.
Count: 10 warps, 60 wefts.
Selvage: no cord, over one warp.

	Fiber	Type of Yarn	Spin	Twist	Ply	Color	Dye
Warp	Wool	Handspun	Z		1	White	Natural
Weft	Wool	Commercial	Z	S	2	Gray	Aniline
	Wool	Commercial	Z	S	2	Royal blue	Aniline
	Wool	Commercial	Z	S	2	White	Natural
	Wool	Commercial	Z	S	2	Black	Aniline
	Wool	Commercial	Z	S	2	Turquoise	Aniline
	Wool	Commercial	Z	S	2	Yellow/ Green	Aniline

185

Rug, Sandpainting
69.67.16

Date: 1960s
Gift of Mr. and Mrs. Edwin L. Kennedy

Beautyway: Sun and Moon.
Red Rock.
Mrs. King Tutt, weaver.

Size: 116 cm. x 114.5 cm.
Count: 14 warps, 56 wefts.
Selvage: no cord, over one warp.

	Fiber	Type of Yarn	Spin	Twist	Ply	Color	Dye
Warp	Wool	Handspun	Z		1	White	Natural
Weft	Wool	Commercial	Z	S	2	Gray/Beige	Aniline
	Wool	Commercial	Z	S	2	Royal blue	Aniline
	Wool	Commercial	Z	S	2	Red	Aniline
	Wool	Commercial	Z	S	2	Yellow	Aniline
	Wool	Commercial	Z	S	2	Black	Aniline
	Wool	Commercial	Z	S	2	White	Natural
	Wool	Commercial	Z	S	2	Brown	Aniline

186

Rug, Sandpainting
69.67.29

Date: 1960s
Gift of Mr. and Mrs. Edwin L. Kennedy

Beautyway: People with Weasel Skins.
Mrs. James Etcitty, weaver.

Size: 148 cm. x 146 cm.
Count: 9 warps, 44 wefts.
Selvage: no cord, over one warp.

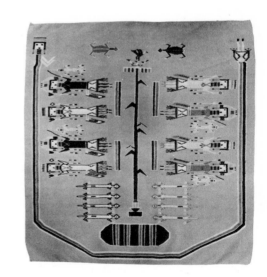

	Fiber	Type of Yarn	Spin	Twist	Ply	Color	Dye
Warp	Wool	Handspun	Z		1	White	Natural
Weft	Wool	Commercial	Z	S	4	White	Natural
	Wool	Commercial	Z	S	4	Peach	Aniline
	Wool	Commercial	Z	S	4	Yellow	Aniline
	Wool	Commercial	Z	S	4	Brown	Aniline
	Wool	Commercial	Z	S	4	Black	Aniline
	Wool	Commercial	Z	S	4	Gray	Aniline

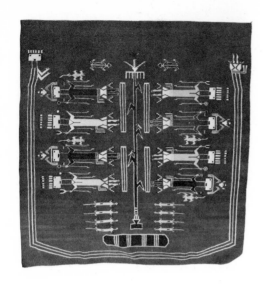

187

Rug, Sandpainting
69.67.30

Date: 1960s
Gift of Mr. and Mrs. Edwin L. Kennedy

Beautyway: People with Weasel Skins.
Red Rock.
Mrs. James Etcitty, weaver.
Size: 145 cm. x 150 cm.
Count: 20 warps, 46 wefts.
Selvage: no cord, over three warps.

	Fiber	Type of Yarn	Spin	Twist	Ply	Color	Dye
Warp	Wool	Handspun	Z		1	White	Natural
Weft	Wool	Handspun	Z		1	White	Natural
	Wool	Handspun	Z		1	Black	Natural+
	Wool	Handspun	Z		1	Med. brown	Natural
	Wool	Handspun	Z		1	Gray	Carded
	Wool	Commercial	Z	S	2	Yellow	Aniline
	Wool	Commercial	Z	S	2	Cocoa	Aniline

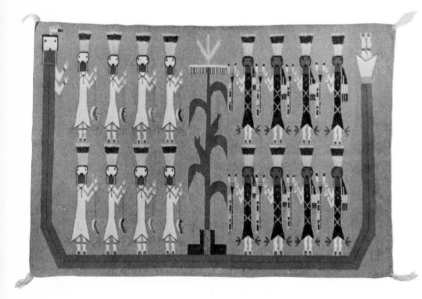

188

Rug, Sandpainting
69.67.31

Date: 1960s
Gift of Mr. and Mrs. Edwin L. Kennedy

Beautyway: People with Weasel Skins
(variation).

Mrs. Tom Peshlakie, weaver.

Size: 166.5 cm. x 111.5 cm.
Count: 15 warps, 40 wefts.
Selvage: no cord, over two twisted warps.

	Fiber	Type of Yarn	Spin	Twist	Ply	Color	Dye
Warp	Wool	Handspun	Z		1	White	Natural
Weft	Wool	Commercial	Z	S	2	White	Natural
	Wool	Commercial	Z	S	4	Black	Aniline
	Wool	Commercial	Z	S	4	Gray	Aniline
	Wool	Commercial	Z	S	4	Turquoise	Aniline
	Wool	Commercial	Z	S	4	Red	Aniline
	Wool	Commercial	Z	S	4	Green	Aniline
	Wool	Commercial	Z	S	4	Yellow	Aniline

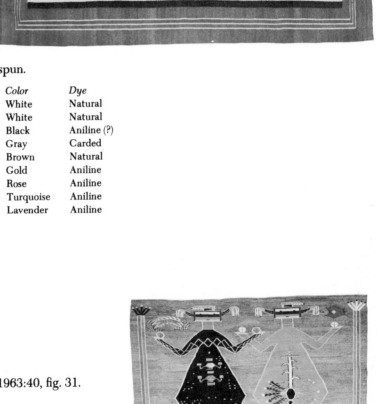

Others

189

Rug, Sandpainting
63.34.131

Date: ca. 1961
Gift of Mr. and Mrs. Gilbert Maxwell

Two Gray Hills (Tohatchi).
Possible adaptation of Mountain Gods.
Patsy Millie, weaver.

Size: 188 cm. x 137.5 cm.
Count: 10 warps, 52 wefts.
Selvage: two cords; 3-ply carded beige handspun.

	Fiber	Type of Yarn	Spin	Twist	Ply	Color	Dye
Warp	Wool	Handspun	Z		1	White	Natural
Weft	Wool	Handspun	Z		1	White	Natural
	Wool	Handspun	Z		1	Black	Aniline (?)
	Wool	Handspun	Z		1	Gray	Carded
	Wool	Handspun	Z		1	Brown	Natural
	Wool	Handspun	Z		1	Gold	Aniline
	Wool	Handspun	Z		1	Rose	Aniline
	Wool	Handspun	Z		1	Turquoise	Aniline
	Wool	Handspun	Z		1	Lavender	Aniline

190

Rug, Sandpainting
63.34.74

Date: 1959
Gift of Mr. and Mrs. Gilbert Maxwell

Two Gray Hills (Tohatchi).
Mother Earth and Father Sky, see Maxwell 1963:40, fig. 31.

Size: 156 cm. x 184.5 cm.
Count: 14 warps, 30 wefts.
Selvage: three cords; 2-ply carded gray handspun.

	Fiber	Type of Yarn	Spin	Twist	Ply	Color	Dye
Warp	Wool	Handspun	Z		1	White	Natural
Weft	Wool	Handspun	Z		1	White	Natural
	Wool	Handspun	Z		1	Black	Aniline
	Wool	Handspun	Z		1	Gray	Carded
	Wool	Handspun	Z		1	Turquoise	Aniline
	Wool	Handspun	Z		1	Rose	Aniline
	Wool	Handspun	Z		1	Yellow/ Green	Aniline

191

Rug, Sandpainting
70.75.9

Date: 1960s
Gift of Mr. and Mrs. Edwin L. Kennedy

Nightway: Water Sprinklers.
Clara Nez, weaver.

Size: 122.5 cm. x 113 cm.
Count: 11 warps, 36 wefts.
Selvage: two cords; 3-ply, each 4-ply aniline dyed rust commercial yarn.

See plate section.

	Fiber	Type of Yarn	Spin	Twist	Ply	Color	Dye
Warp	Wool	Handspun	Z		1	White	Natural
Weft	Wool	Commercial	Z	S	4	White	Natural
	Wool	Commercial	Z	S	4	Black	Aniline
	Wool	Commercial	Z	S	4	Gray	Aniline
	Wool	Commercial	Z	S	4	Mottled gray	Aniline
	Wool	Commercial	Z	S	4	Blue	Aniline
	Wool	Commercial	Z	S	4	Turquoise	Aniline
	Wool	Commercial	Z	S	4	Red	Aniline
	Wool	Commercial	Z	S	4	Maroon	Aniline
	Wool	Commercial	Z	S	4	Gold	Aniline
	Wool	Commercial	Z	S	4	Yellow	Aniline
	Wool	Commercial	Z	S	4	Rust	Aniline

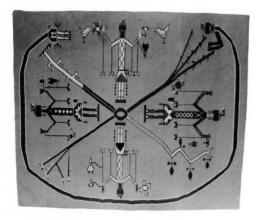

192

Rug, Sandpainting
70.75.6

Date: 1960s
Gift of Mr. and Mrs. Edwin L. Kennedy

Perhaps from Windway.
Vera Begay, weaver.

Size: 186 cm. x 152.5 cm.
Count: 14 warps, 52 wefts.
Selvage: three cords; 2-ply natural white handspun.

	Fiber	Type of Yarn	Spin	Twist	Ply	Color	Dye
Warp	Wool	Handspun	Z		1	White	Natural
Weft	Wool	Commercial	Z	S	3	Gray/Beige	Aniline
	Wool	Commercial	Z	S	3	Black	Aniline
	Wool	Commercial	Z	S	3	White	Natural
	Wool	Commercial	Z	S	3	Red	Aniline
	Wool	Commercial	Z	S	3	Brown	Aniline
	Wool	Commercial	Z	S	3	Royal blue	Aniline
	Wool	Commercial	Z	S	3	Yellow	Aniline
	Wool	Commercial	Z	S	3	Turquoise	Aniline

193

Rug, Sandpainting
63.34.129

Date: ca. 1961

Gift of Mr. and Mrs. Gilbert Maxwell

Shooting Way, Female Branch: Sun with figure of Nayenez-
gani. Copy of a painting by Hosteen Nez.
Shiprock.

Mrs. Tom Peshlakai, weaver.

Size: 126.5 cm. x 100.5 cm.

Count: 11 warps, 32 wefts.

Selvage: no cord, over one warp.

	Fiber	Type of Yarn	Spin	Twist	Ply	Color	Dye
Warp	Wool	Handspun	Z	S	2	White	Natural
Weft	Wool	Commercial	Z	S	3	White	Natural
	Wool	Commercial	Z	S	3	Black	Aniline
	Wool	Commercial	Z	S	3	Gray	Aniline
	Wool	Commercial	Z	S	3	Turquoise	Aniline
	Wool	Commercial	Z	S	3	Orange	Aniline
	Wool	Commercial	Z	S	3	Yellow	Aniline
	Wool	Commercial	Z	S	3	Bright pink	Aniline

194

Rug, Sandpainting
70.75.8

Date: 1960s

Gift of Mr. and Mrs. Edwin L. Kennedy

Rainbow People. Could be from any of six different chants:
Mountain, Beauty, Plume, Wind, Male Shooting, or Night.
Mary Lewis, weaver.

Size: 151 cm. x 143 cm.

Count: 13 warps, 50 wefts.

Selvage: no cord, over one warp.

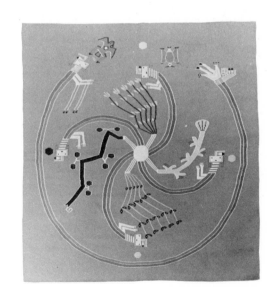

	Fiber	Type of Yarn	Spin	Twist	Ply	Color	Dye
Warp	Cotton	String				White	Natural
Weft	Wool	Commercial	Z	S	2	White	Natural
	Wool	Commercial	Z	S	2	Black	Aniline
	Wool	Commercial	Z	S	2	Med. brown	Aniline
	Wool	Commercial	Z	S	2	Red	Aniline
	Wool	Commercial	Z	S	2	Yellow	Aniline
	Wool	Commercial	Z	S	2	Med. blue	Aniline

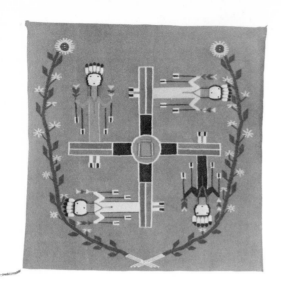

195

Rug, Sandpainting
69.67.19

Date: 1960s
Gift of Mr. and Mrs. Edwin L. Kennedy

Big God Way: Sun Flower People.
May Rose Tyler, weaver.

Size: 111 cm. x 114 cm.
Count: 10 warps, 44 wefts.
Selvage: no cord, over one warp.

	Fiber	Type of Yarn	Spin	Twist	Ply	Color	Dye
Warp	Wool	Handspun	Z	S	2	White	Natural
Weft	Wool	Commercial	Z	S	4	White	Natural
	Wool	Commercial	Z	S	4	Black	Aniline
	Wool	Commercial	Z	S	4	Green	Aniline
	Wool	Commercial	Z	S	4	Rust brown	Aniline
	Wool	Commercial	Z	S	4	Turquoise	Aniline
	Wool	Commercial	Z	S	4	Red	Aniline
	Wool	Commercial	Z	S	4	Royal blue	Aniline
	Wool	Commercial	Z	S	4	Yellow	Aniline
	Wool	Commercial	Z	S	4	Light blue	Aniline
	Wool	Commercial	Z	S	4	Pink	Aniline

196

Rug, Sandpainting
70.75.5

Date: 1960s
Gift of Mr. and Mrs. Edwin L. Kennedy

Red Rock.
Mrs. King Tutt, weaver.

Size: 139 cm. x 141 cm.
Count: 12 warps, 56 wefts.
Selvage: no cord, over one warp.

	Fiber	Type of Yarn	Spin	Twist	Ply	Color	Dye
Warp	Wool	Handspun	Z		1	White	Natural
Weft	Wool	Commercial	Z	S	2	White	Natural
	Wool	Commercial	Z	S	2	Beige	Aniline
	Wool	Commercial	Z	S	2	Black	Aniline
	Wool	Commercial	Z	S	2	Bright pink	Aniline
	Wool	Commercial	Z	S	2	Green	Aniline
	Wool	Commercial	Z	S	2	Yellow	Aniline
	Wool	Commercial	Z	S	2	Mint green	Aniline
	Wool	Commercial	Z	S	2	Turquoise	Aniline
	Wool	Commercial	Z	S	2	Purple	Aniline
	Wool	Commercial	Z	S	2	Red	Aniline
	Wool	Commercial	Z	S	2	Royal blue	Aniline

197

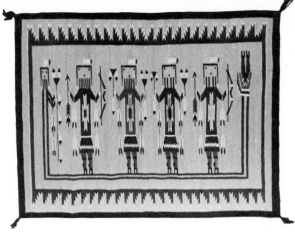

Rug, Sandpainting
75.324.1

Date: 1966–67
Gift of Mr. and Mrs. Gilbert Maxwell
Shiprock.
Lucy Chase, weaver.
Won first prize and Special United Indian
Traders Award at the Gallup Ceremonial in 1967.

Size: 117.5 cm. x 87.5 cm.
Count: 9 warps, 52 wefts.
Selvage: two cords; 2-ply, each ply a strand of 4-ply aniline
dyed black commercial yarn.

	Fiber	Type of Yarn	Spin	Twist	Ply	Color	Dye
Warp	Wool	Handspun	Z		1	White	Natural
Weft	Wool	Handspun	Z		1	White	Natural
	Wool	Handspun	Z		1	Black	Aniline
	Wool	Handspun	Z		1	Brown	Natural
	Wool	Handspun	Z		1	Beige	Carded
	Wool	Handspun	Z		1	Gray	Carded
	Wool	Handspun	Z		1	Gold/ Brown	Vegetal
	Wool	Handspun	Z		1	Gold	Vegetal

198

Rug, Sandpainting
63.34.148

Date: ca. 1957
Gift of Mr. and Mrs. Gilbert Maxwell

Perhaps adaptation of Mountain Gods,
see Maxwell 1963:34, fig. 20.
Formerly in Don Watson Collection.

Size: 149 cm. x 91.5 cm.
Count: 9 warps, 30 wefts.
Selvage: no cord, two warps twisted together.

	Fiber	Type of Yarn	Spin	Twist	Ply	Color	Dye
Warp	Wool	Handspun	Z		1	White	Natural
Weft	Wool	Handspun	Z		1	White	Natural
	Wool		Z		1	Black	Aniline
	Wool	Handspun	Z		1	Gray	Aniline
	Wool	Handspun	Z		1	Beige	Aniline
	Wool	Handspun	Z		1	Purple	Aniline
	Wool	Handspun	Z		1	Dark blue	Aniline
	Wool	Handspun	Z		1	Red	Aniline
	Wool	Handspun	Z		1	Dark green	Aniline
	Wool	Handspun	Z		1	Med. green	Aniline
	Wool	Handspun	Z		1	Olive green	Aniline
	Wool	Handspun	Z		1	Chartreuse	Aniline
	Wool	Handspun	Z		1	Med. brown	Aniline

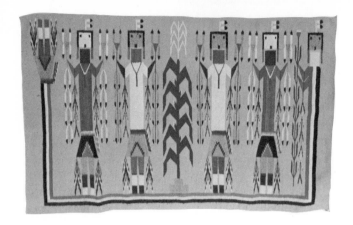

199

Rug, Sandpainting
63.34.71

Date: 1956–57

Gift of Mr. and Mrs. Gilbert Maxwell

Farmington area.
Dorothy Funston, weaver.
Won second prize at Gallup Ceremonial in 1957.

Size: 127 cm. x 76 cm.

Count: 12 warps, 50 wefts.

Selvage: no cord, over one warp.

	Fiber	Type of Yarn	Spin	Twist	Ply	Color	Dye
Warp	Wool	Handspun	Z		1	White	Natural
Weft	Wool	Commercial	Z	S	2	White	Natural
	Wool	Commercial	Z	S	2	Peach	Aniline
	Wool	Commercial	Z	S	2	Black	Aniline
	Wool	Commercial	Z	S	2	Red	Aniline
	Wool	Commercial	Z	S	2	Turquoise	Aniline
	Wool	Commercial	Z	S	2	Purple	Aniline
	Wool	Commercial	Z	S	2	Pink	Aniline
	Wool	Commercial	Z	S	2	Gray	Aniline
	Wool	Commercial	Z	S	2	Green	Aniline
	Wool	Commercial	Z	S	2	Yellow	Aniline
	Wool	Handspun	Z		1	Beige	Carded

Miscellaneous Garments

200

Handbag
63.34.188

Date: ca. 1960

Gift of Mr. and Mrs. Gilbert Maxwell

Handbag with inner pocket, buttonholed flap and handle all woven in one piece and sewn down the sides.

Size: 31.5 cm. x 29 cm.

Count: 8 warps, 20 wefts.

Selvage: no cord, over two warps.

	Fiber	Type of Yarn	Spin	Twist	Ply	Color	Dye
Warp	Cotton	String				White	Natural
Weft	Wool	Handspun	Z		1	White	Natural
	Wool	Handspun	Z		1	Black	Aniline
	Wool	Handspun	Z		1	Orange	Aniline
	Wool	Handspun	Z		1	Gold	Aniline

Note: Gold appears only in one stripe hidden inside.

201

Jacket
63.34.177

Date: ca. 1960

Gift of Mr. and Mrs. Gilbert Maxwell

Sleeves and collar woven separately and sewn on.

Size: 57 cm. x 49 cm.

Count: 9 warps, 32 wefts.

Selvage: two cords; 3-ply brown natural handspun.

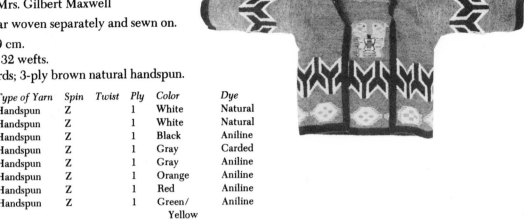

	Fiber	Type of Yarn	Spin	Twist	Ply	Color	Dye
Warp	Wool	Handspun	Z		1	White	Natural
Weft	Wool	Handspun	Z		1	White	Natural
	Wool	Handspun	Z		1	Black	Aniline
	Wool	Handspun	Z		1	Gray	Carded
	Wool	Handspun	Z		1	Gray	Aniline
	Wool	Handspun	Z		1	Orange	Aniline
	Wool	Handspun	Z		1	Red	Aniline
	Wool	Handspun	Z		1	Green/ Yellow	Aniline

Note: Goat hair carded in.

Navajo- and Pueblo-made warp float belts appear to be technically identical and most in the Maxwell Museum collection have been placed in the Pueblo section. Those included here were identified as Navajo-made by their donors.

202

Belt
55.20.41

Date: ca. 1880

Gift of Mrs. Richard Wetherill

Worn by Mrs. Wetherill at a Corn Dance in 1885–86.
Warp float weave.

Size: 108.5 cm. x 7.5 cm.

Count: 15 warps, 68 wefts.

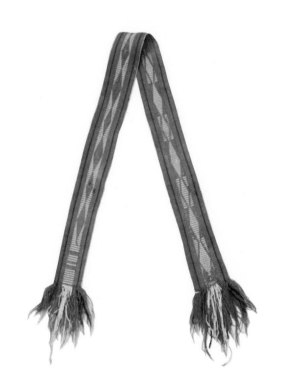

	Fiber	Type of Yarn	Spin	Twist	Ply	Color	Dye
Warp	Wool	Commercial	Z	S	4	Red	Aniline
	Wool	Commercial	Z	S	4	Blue	Aniline
	Cotton	String				White	Natural
Weft	Cotton	String				White	Natural

203
Belt
55.20.40

Date: 1880–1900
Gift of Mrs. Richard Wetherill

Warp float weave.

Size: 67 cm. x 7 cm.
Count: 17 warps, 60 wefts.

	Fiber	Type of Yarn	Spin	Twist	Ply	Color	Dye
Warp	Wool	Commercial	Z	S	4	Red	Aniline
	Wool	Commercial	Z	S	4	Med. green	Aniline
	Wool	Commercial	Z	S	4	Acid green	Aniline
	Wool	Commercial	Z	S	4	Purple	Aniline
	Cotton	String				White	Natural
Weft	Cotton	String				White	Natural

Note: Cotton string is fine like a sewing cotton.

204
Belt
55.20.38

Date: 1880–1900
Gift of Mrs. Richard Wetherill

Warp float weave.

Size: 80 cm. x 6.5 cm.
Count: 20 warps, 64 wefts.

	Fiber	Type of Yarn	Spin	Twist	Ply	Color	Dye
Warp	Wool	Handspun	Z	S	2	Red	Aniline
	Wool	Handspun	Z	S	2	Faded blue	Aniline
	Cotton	String				White	Natural
Weft	Cotton	String				White	Natural

205
Belt
55.20.39

Date: 1880–1900
Gift of Mrs. Richard Wetherill

Warp float weave.

Size: 73 cm. x 6 cm.
Count: 14 warps, 36 wefts.

	Fiber	Type of Yarn	Spin	Twist	Ply	Color	Dye
Warp	Wool	Commercial	Z	S	4	Red	Aniline
	Wool	Commercial	Z	S	4	Purple	Aniline
	Cotton	String				White	Natural
Weft	Cotton	String				White	Natural

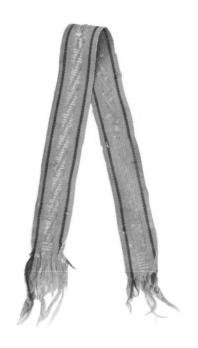

206
Belt
55.20.42

Date: 1880–1900
Gift of Mrs. Richard Wetherill

Warp float weave.

Size: 221.5 cm. x 10 cm.
Count: 12 warps, 40 wefts.

	Fiber	Type of Yarn	Spin	Twist	Ply	Color	Dye
Warp	Wool	Commercial	Z	S	4	Red	Aniline
	Wool	Commercial	Z	S	4	Green	Aniline
	Cotton	String				White	Natural
Weft	Cotton	String				White	Natural

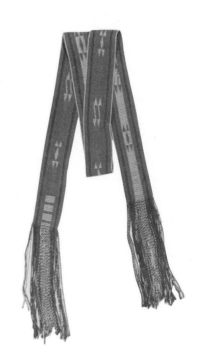

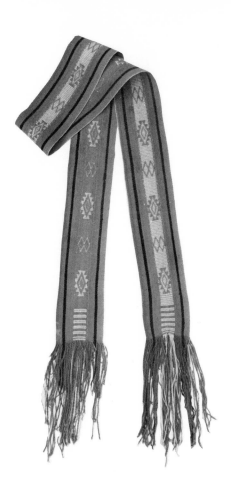

207
Belt
68.46.48

Date: 1880–1900
Indefinite loan from Mr. and Mrs. Gilbert Maxwell

Size: 200 cm. x 12 cm.
Count: 12 warps, 48 wefts.

	Fiber	Type of Yarn	Spin	Twist	Ply	Color	Dye
Warp	Wool	Commercial	Z	S	4	Red	Aniline
	Wool	Handspun	Z	S	2	Dark blue	Indigo
	Cotton	String				White	Natural
Weft	Cotton	String				White	Natural

2
PUEBLO TEXTILES

The ancestors of the modern Pueblo Indians began to use the large upright loom around A.D. 800 (Wheat:1975). Pueblo weaving traditions are not only much older than those of the Navajo but are much more complicated. While a tapestry weave is the most common Navajo technique, twills, 50/50 plain weaves, and warp faced weaves are the usual Pueblo techniques. These weaves produce fabrics that make a suitable background for embroidery.

Pueblo men traditionally weave and embroider except at Zuni where the women do this work. Unlike the Navajo the Pueblos did not convert their blanket weaving tradition to a rug weaving one and their weaving has always been for Indian use. The introduction of white manufactured clothing has radically reduced the quantity of Pueblo weaving: traditional garments have been replaced by industrially made goods for everyday wear and only the need for ceremonial costumes has kept Pueblo weaving alive. Even so, almost no weaving is done at the Rio Grande Pueblos and most Pueblo textiles of the last sixty years have been made at Hopi for sale and trade to other villages.

In this section of the catalog the textiles are divided according to their function as men's or women's clothing. The basic woman's garment is the manta which does double duty as a shawl thrown over the shoulders or as a dress when sewn up the side. Frequently the plain white wedding manta, presented by the groom for the wedding ceremony, was later embroidered along the top and bottom.

Traditional men's garments represented in the Museum's collection are the kilt, sash, shoulder blanket, shirt, stockings, and leggings. Kilts are generally embroidered while sashes are executed in a wrapped brocade technique giving the appearance of embroidery. The main fabric of a sash is cotton with wool decoration floated over its face and wrapped around approximately every seventh warp. The design of the sash is always the same, a stylized head of the Broadfaced Kachina.

Small belts in the warp float technique are commonly woven today and are frequently worn as a belt on a modern European style dress.

Women's Garments

1

Manta
71.26.1

Date: 1870–80
Gift of Mr. Tom Bahti

Acoma?
Diagonal twill with red and green embroidery in strips at the top and bottom.

Size: 111 cm. x 146 cm.
Selvage: three cords; 2-ply black natural+ handspun.

	Fiber	Type of Yarn	Spin	Twist	Ply	Color	Dye
Warp	Wool	Handspun	Z		1	Black	Natural+
Weft	Wool	Handspun	Z		1	Black	Natural+
Embroidery	Wool	Handspun	Z		1	Yellow/Green	Aniline
	Wool	Raveled	Z	S	2	Red	Aniline

2

Manta
70.56.1

Date: 1870–80
Gift of Mr. and Mrs. Bruce T. Ellis

Hopi?
Warp face weave with embroidery.

Size: 99 cm. x 127 cm.
Count: 30 warps, 18 wefts.

Selvage: three cords; 2-ply natural white handspun cotton.

	Fiber	Type of Yarn	Spin	Twist	Ply	Color	Dye
Warp	Cotton	Handspun	Z		1	White	Natural
Weft	Cotton	Handspun	Z		1	White	Natural

Note: Warp thread has a tighter spin than the weft.

	Fiber	Type of Yarn	Spin	Twist	Ply	Color	Dye
Embroidery	Wool	Handspun	S	Z	2	Yellow	Vegetal (?)
	Wool	Handspun	S	Z	2	Black	Vegetal
	Wool	Raveled	Z	S	2	Red	Cochineal

See plate section.

116

3

Manta

63.34.136

Date: 1880–1900

Gift of Mr. and Mrs. Gilbert Maxwell

Zuni.

Diagonal twill with wide bands of embroidery along top and bottom and narrow strips along sides. When the black first faded the entire dress was redyed, thus giving the embroidery a black cast.

Size: 104 cm. x 149.5 cm.

Selvage: three cords; 2-ply natural+ black handspun. Note: wool rings instead of tassels on the corners.

	Fiber	Type of Yarn	Spin	Twist	Ply	Color	Dye
Warp	Wool	Handspun	Z		1	Black	Natural+
Weft	Wool	Handspun	Z		1	Black	Natural+
Embroidery	Wool	Handspun	Z		1	Blue	Indigo
	Wool	Handspun	Z	S	2	Blue	Indigo

4

Dress

63.34.137

Date: 1880–1900

Gift of Mr. and Mrs. Gilbert Maxwell

Zuni.

Diagonal twill weave with embroidery along top and bottom edges and narrower bands of embroidery along the sides. The two parts of the dress are sewn together halfway down the edge with red yarn. When the black first faded the entire dress was redyed, thus giving the embroidery a black cast.

Size: 113.5 cm. x 131.5 cm.

Selvage: three cords; 2-ply natural+ black handspun. Note: no tassels on the corners but wool rings instead.

	Fiber	Type of Yarn	Spin	Twist	Ply	Color	Dye
Warp	Wool	Handspun	Z		1	Black	Natural+
Weft	Wool	Handspun	Z		1	Black	Natural+
Embroidery	Wool	Handspun	Z		1	Blue	Indigo
	Wool	Handspun	Z	S	2	Blue	Indigo

5
Skirt
75.322.4

Date: ca. 1940
Gift of Mr. and Mrs. Gilbert Maxwell

Jemez.
Made for Mrs. Maxwell's initiation into the Jemez Tribe. It forms a costume with the following blouse.
Juanita Lee, maker.

Size: 75 cm. in length.
The skirt is commercial cloth but the embroidery is done by hand.

	Fiber	Type of Yarn	Spin	Twist	Ply	Color	Dye
Embroidery	Wool	Commercial	Z	S	4	Shocking pink	Aniline
	Wool	Commercial	Z	S	4	Turquoise	Aniline
	Wool	Commercial	Z	S	4	Yellow	Aniline

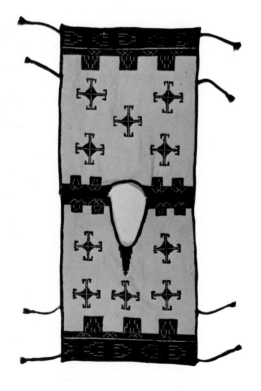

6
Blouse
75.322.5

Date: ca. 1940
Gift of Mr. and Mrs. Gilbert Maxwell

Jemez.
Made for Mrs. Maxwell's initiation into the Jemez Tribe. It forms a costume with the preceding skirt.
The blouse is woven in two pieces and sewn together at the shoulders.
Plain weave.

Size: 56.5 cm. x 48 cm.

	Fiber	Type of Yarn	Spin	Twist	Ply	Color	Dye
Warp	Cotton	Handspun	Z		1	White	Natural
Weft	Cotton	Handspun	Z		1	White	Natural
Embroidery	Wool	Commercial	Z	S	4	Dark blue	Aniline
	Wool	Commercial	Z	S	4	Red	Aniline

7

Manta

63.34.138

Date: 1880–1900

Gift of Mr. and Mrs. Gilbert Maxwell

Zuni?

Diagonal twill with diamond twill in blue at top and bottom.
Thick bands of plain embroidery added at inner edges of borders: blue, yellow extend all the way across and red one-fifth of the way in on either side.

Size: 103 cm. x 130 cm.

Selvage: three cords; 2-ply indigo dyed handspun.

	Fiber	Type of Yarn	Spin	Twist	Ply	Color	Dye
Warp	Wool	Handspun	Z		1	Dark brown	Natural
Weft	Wool	Handspun	Z		1	Dark brown	Natural
	Wool	Handspun	Z		1	Blue	Indigo
Embroidery	Wool	Handspun	Z	S	2	Blue	Indigo
	Wool	Handspun	Z	S	2	Yellow	Vegetal
	Wool	Commercial	Z	S	4	Red	Cochineal (?)
	Wool	Commercial	Z	S	4	Yellow	Vegetal

Note: Some of the 4-ply red embroidery yarn is used in pairs.

8

Dress

61.3.506

Date: 1880–1900

Gift of Mrs. Joseph Imhof, the
Joseph Imhof Collection

Zuni.

Diagonal twill with diamond twill in blue at top and bottom.
The dress still has the original stitching holding it together on the shoulder.

Size: 97 cm. x 125.5 cm.

Selvage: two cords; 2-ply indigo dyed handspun.

	Fiber	Type of Yarn	Spin	Twist	Ply	Color	Dye
Warp	Wool	Handspun	Z	S	2	Black	Natural+
Weft	Wool	Handspun	Z		1	Black	Natural+
	Wool	Handspun	Z		1	Blue	Indigo

9

Manta
76.1.38

Date: ca. 1950
Donor unknown

Hopi.
Plain and diagonal twill weave.

Size: 84.5 cm. x 92 cm.

Selvage: three cords; 2-ply aniline dyed black handspun.

	Fiber	Type of Yarn	Spin	Twist	Ply	Color	Dye
Warp	Cotton	String				White	Natural
Weft	Wool	Handspun	Z	S	2	Red	Aniline
	Wool	Handspun	Z	S	2	Black	Aniline
	Cotton	Handspun	Z		1	White	Natural
	Cotton	String				White	Natural

10

Manta
67.126.2

Date: 1950–60
Gift of Mr. and Mrs. Gilbert Maxwell
Hopi.
Diagonal and plain twill weave.

Size: 94 cm. x 132.5 cm.

Selvage: three cords; each two strands of 3-ply aniline dyed blue commercial yarn.

	Fiber	Type of Yarn	Spin	Twist	Ply	Color	Dye
Warp	Cotton	String				White	Natural
Weft	Cotton	String				White	Natural
	Cotton	Handspun	Z		1	White	Natural
	Wool	Commercial	Z	S	3	Red	Aniline
	Wool	Commercial	Z	S	3	Blue	Aniline

11

Wedding Manta
67.126.1

Date: 1940–60
Gift of Mr. and Mrs. Gilbert Maxwell

Hopi.
"E. Chapalla" in ink on one edge.
Warp-faced weave.

Size: 105.5 cm. x 157 cm.
Count: 32 warps, 11 wefts.
Selvage: three cords; 3-ply natural white handspun cotton.

	Fiber	Type of Yarn	Spin	Twist	Ply	Color	Dye
Warp	Cotton	String				White	Natural
Weft	Cotton	Handspun	Z		1	White	Natural

12

Child's Wedding Manta
71.33.3

Date: 1971
Acquired from the Museum of Northern Arizona

Hopi, Kiakochomovi.
Frances Alpeche, weaver.
Warp-faced weave with single line of embroidery in the four corners and two large tassels, one with a small feather tied in.

Size: 76 cm. x 107.5 cm.
Count: 26 warps, 8 wefts.
Selvage: three cords; 2-ply white handspun cotton.

	Fiber	Type of Yarn	Spin	Twist	Ply	Color	Dye
Warp	Cotton	String				White	Natural
Weft	Cotton	Handspun	Z		1	White	Natural
Embroidery	Wool	Handspun	Z		1	Orange/ Brown	Ochre (?)

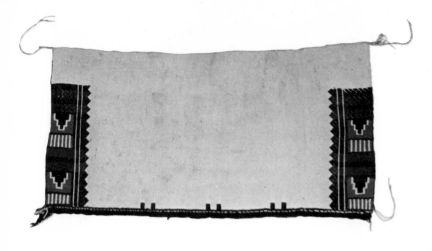

Men's Garments

13

Kilt
63.34.171
Date: ca. 1910
Gift of Mr. and Mrs. Gilbert Maxwell
Plain weave with embroidery.

Size: 53 cm. x 111 cm.
Count: 15 warps, 30 wefts.
Selvage: four cords; white cotton string.

	Fiber	Type of Yarn	Spin	Twist	Ply	Color	Dye
Warp	Cotton	Handspun	Z		1	White	Natural
Weft	Cotton	String				White	Natural
Embroidery	Wool	Commercial	Z	S	4	Red	Aniline
	Wool	Commercial	Z	S	4	Green	Aniline
	Wool	Commercial	Z	S	4	Black	Aniline

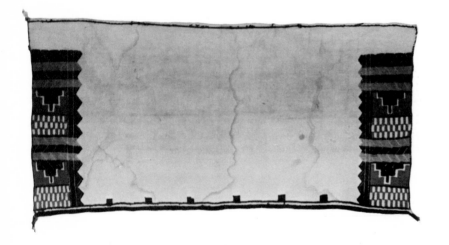

14

Kilt
61.3.619
Date: 1900–20
Gift of Mrs. Joseph Imhof, the
Joseph Imhof Collection

Identified as Cochiti by Mr. Imhof.
Plain weave with embroidered ends
and a black braided border sewn on.

Size: 105.5 cm. x 50 cm.
Count: 16 warps, 18 wefts.
Selvage: completely hemmed.

	Fiber	Type of Yarn	Spin	Twist	Ply	Color	Dye
Warp	Cotton	Handspun	Z		1	White	Natural
Weft	Cotton	Handspun	Z		1	White	Natural
Embroidery	Wool	Commercial	Z	S	4	Red	Aniline
	Wool	Commercial	Z	S	4	Black	Aniline
	Wool	Commercial	Z	S	4	Green	Aniline

15

Kilt
61.3.618

Date: 1900–20
Gift of Mrs. Joseph Imhof, the
Joseph Imhof Collection

Identified as Cochiti by Mr. Imhof.
Plain weave with embroidery and a
green wool braided border sewn on.

Size: 103.5 cm. x 46 cm.
Count: 14 warps, 22 wefts.
Selvage: completely hemmed.

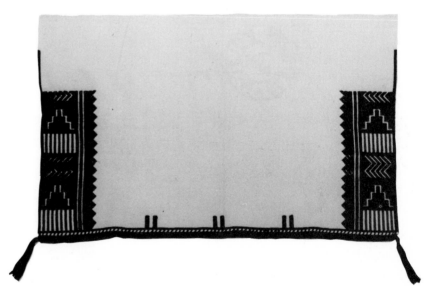

	Fiber	Type of Yarn	Spin	Twist	Ply	Color	Dye
Warp	Cotton	Handspun	Z	S	2	White	Natural
Weft	Cotton	Handspun	Z	S	1	White	Natural
Embroi-dery	Wool	Commercial	Z	S	4	Black	Aniline
	Wool	Commercial	Z	S	4	Red	Aniline
	Wool	Commercial	Z	S	4	Gray	Aniline
	Wool	Commercial	Z	S	4	Green	Aniline

16

Kilt
66.89.1

Date: 1950–60
Gift of Mr. and Mrs. Bruce T. Ellis

Hopi.
Jeanette Lamabuma, maker.
Commercial cotton cloth, marked "Fulton Seamless" with
embroidered ends and a black braided edging.

Size: 107 cm. x 63 cm.

	Fiber	Type of Yarn	Spin	Twist	Ply	Color	Dye
Embroi-dery	Wool	Commercial	Z	S	4	Black	Aniline
	Wool	Commercial	Z	S	4	Red	Aniline
	Wool	Commercial	Z	S	4	Green	Aniline

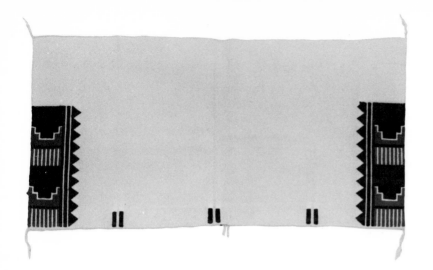

17

Kilt

76.1.37

Date: ca. 1950
Donor unknown

Hopi.
Warp faced weave with embroidery.

Size: 125 cm. x 63 cm.
Count: 24 warps, 10 wefts.

Selvage: two cords; 2-ply natural white handspun cotton.

	Fiber	Type of Yarn	Spin	Twist	Ply	Color	Dye
Warp	Cotton	String				White	Natural
Weft	Wool	Commercial	Z	S	4	White	Natural
Embroi-dery	Wool	Commercial	Z	S	4	Red	Aniline
	Wool	Commercial	Z	S	4	Black	Aniline
	Wool	Commercial	Z	S	4	Green	Aniline

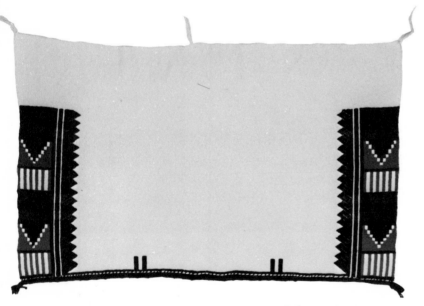

18

Kilt

67.33.6

Date: ca. 1950
Purchase

Hopi.
Warp faced weave with embroidery
and a braided edging.

Size: 117 cm. x 69 cm.
Count: 32 warps, 12 wefts.

Selvage: three cords; 2-ply natural white cotton handspun.

	Fiber	Type of Yarn	Spin	Twist	Ply	Color	Dye
Warp	Cotton	String				White	Natural
Weft	Cotton	Handspun	Z		1	White	Natural
Embroi-dery	Wool	Commercial	Z	S	4	Black	Aniline
	Wool	Commercial	Z	S	4	Red	Aniline
	Wool	Commercial	Z	S	4	Green	Aniline

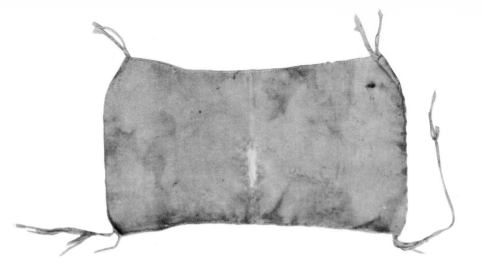

19

Boy's Kilt
66.107.2

Date: 1920–50
Gift of Mrs. T. W. Ewing

Hopi.
Warp faced weave.

Size: 53.5 cm. x 30 cm.
Count: 26 warps, 12 wefts.
Selvage: three cords; 2-ply natural white handspun cotton.

	Fiber	Type of Yarn	Spin	Twist	Ply	Color	Dye
Warp	Cotton	String				White	Natural
Weft	Cotton	Handspun	Z		1	White	Natural

20

Half of a Sash
55.20.5a

Date: ca. 1900
Gift of Mrs. Richard Wetherill

Hopi.
Forms a complete sash with 55.20.5b.
Warp faced weave with wrapped brocading and long braided warp fringe.

Size: 99 cm. x 23 cm.
Count: 28 warps, 8 wefts.
Selvage: two cords; 4-ply aniline dyed green commercial yarn.

	Fiber	Type of Yarn	Spin	Twist	Ply	Color	Dye
Warp	Cotton	String				White	Natural
Weft	Cotton	String				White	Natural
	Wool	Handspun	Z		1	White	Natural
Bro-cading	Wool	Commercial	Z	S	4	Red	Aniline
	Wool	Commercial	Z	S	4	Green	Aniline
	Wool	Commercial	Z	S	4	Black	Aniline
	Wool	Commercial	Z	S	3	Purple	Aniline

21

Half of a Sash
55.20.5b

Date: ca. 1900
Gift of Mrs. Richard Wetherill

Hopi.
Forms a complete sash with 55.20.5a.
Size: 98 cm. x 22 cm.

22

Sash

61.3.162

Date: 1900–20

Gift of Mrs. Joseph Imhof, the
Joseph Imhof Collection

Identified as Cochiti by Mr. Imhof.
Two separately woven pieces sewn together.
Warp-faced weave with wrapped brocading, a knotted warp fringe, and red silk ribbon sewn on.

Size: 218 cm. (both pieces) x 28.5 cm.

Count: 14 warps, 18 wefts.

Selvage: two cords; each 4-ply aniline dyed yarn, one green and one red.

	Fiber	Type of Yarn	Spin	Twist	Ply	Color	Dye
Warp	Cotton	String				White	Natural
Weft	Cotton	String				White	Natural
	Cotton	Handspun	Z		1	White	Natural
Bro-							
cading	Wool	Commercial	Z	S	4	Red	Aniline
	Wool	Commercial	Z	S	4	Black	Aniline
	Wool	Commercial	Z	S	4	Green	Aniline
	Wool	Commercial	Z	S	4	Purple	Aniline

23

Half of a Sash

61.3.163

Date: 1880–1900

Gift of Mrs. Joseph Imhof, the
Joseph Imhof Collection

Identified as Cochiti by Mr. Imhof.
Warp faced weave with wrapped brocading and warp fringe.
This forms a complete sash with 61.3.165.

Size: 106 cm. x 28.5 cm.

Count: 26 warps, 7 wefts.

Selvage: two cords; 1-ply natural white handspun wool.

	Fiber	Type of Yarn	Spin	Twist	Ply	Color	Dye
Warp	Wool	Handspun	Z		1	White	Natural
Weft	Wool	Handspun	Z		1	White	Natural
Bro-							
cading	Wool	Handspun	Z		1	Black	Natural+
	Wool	Handspun	Z		1	Yellow	Vegetal
	Wool	Handspun	Z	S	2	Blue	Indigo
	Wool	Commercial	Z	S	3	Red	Cochineal

24

Half of a Sash
61.3.165

Date: 1880–1900
Gift of Mrs. Joseph Imhof, the
Joseph Imhof Collection

This forms a complete piece with 61.3.163.

Size: 110 cm. x 28.5 cm.
Count: 22 warps, 8 wefts.
Selvage: two cords; 2-ply natural white handspun wool.

25

Half of a Sash
61.3.481

Date: 1900–20
Gift of Mrs. Joseph Imhof, the
Joseph Imhof Collection

Hopi.
Warp faced weave with wrapped brocading and warp fringe.

Size: 102.5 cm. x 28 cm.
Count: 18 warps, 9 wefts.
Selvage: two cords; 2-ply each ply a piece of aniline dyed red
        commercial yarn.

	Fiber	Type of Yarn	Spin	Twist	Ply	Color	Dye
Warp	Cotton	String				White	Natural
Weft	Cotton	String				White	Natural
	Wool	Commercial	Z	S	4	White	Natural
Bro-cading	Wool	Commercial	Z	S	4	Black	Aniline
	Wool	Commercial	Z	S	4	Green	Aniline
	Wool	Commercial	Z	S	4	Red	Aniline
	Wool	Commercial	Z	S	4	Purple	Aniline

26

Half of a Sash
61.3.164

Date: 1880–1900
Gift of Mrs. Joseph Imhof, the
Joseph Imhof Collection

Identified as Cochiti by Mr. Imhof.
Warp faced weave with wrapped brocading and warp fringe.
Two pieces of red flannel sewn on—one on either side of brocading.

Size: 101 cm. x 31 cm.
Count: 24 warps, 13 wefts.
Selvage: two cords; 2-ply vegetal dyed handspun, one white, one yellow.

	Fiber	Type of Yarn	Spin	Twist	Ply	Color	Dye
Warp	Wool	Handspun	Z		1	White	Natural
Weft	Wool	Handspun	Z		1	White	Natural
Bro-cading	Wool	Commercial	Z	S	3	Red	Aniline
	Wool	Handspun	Z		1	Black	Aniline
	Wool	Handspun	Z		1	Blue	Aniline
	Wool	Handspun	Z		1	Green	Aniline

27

Half of a Sash
61.3.166

Date: 1880–1900
Gift of Mrs. Joseph Imhof, the
Joseph Imhof Collection

Forms a complete sash with preceding piece.

Size: 99 cm. x 28 cm.
Count: 24 warps, 13 wefts.

28

Sash

67.126.3

Date: ca. 1950

Gift of Mr. and Mrs. Gilbert Maxwell

Hopi.

Warp faced weave with wrapped brocading and a warp fringe. Two halves laced together.

Size: 214 cm. (both halves) x 25.5 cm.

Count: 18 warps, 12 wefts.

Selvage: two cords; 2-ply, each 4-ply aniline dyed commercial yarn, one cord red and one green.

	Fiber	Type of Yarn	Spin	Twist	Ply	Color	Dye
Warp	Cotton	String				White	Natural
Weft	Cotton	String				White	Natural
	Wool	Commercial	Z	S	4	White	Natural
Bro-cading	Wool	Commercial	Z	S	4	Red	Aniline
	Wool	Commercial	Z	S	4	Black	Aniline
	Wool	Commercial	Z	S	4	Green	Aniline
	Wool	Commercial	Z	S	4	Purple	Aniline

29

Sash

74.28.21

Date: ca. 1950

Donor unknown

Hopi.

Warp faced weave with wrapped brocading and a warp fringe. Strip of red baize sewn on above fringe.

Size: 212 cm. x 29 cm.

Count: 14 warps, 10 wefts.

Selvage: two cords; 2-ply, each ply a strand of 4-ply aniline dyed commercial yarn, one strand red, one green.

	Fiber	Type of Yarn	Spin	Twist	Ply	Color	Dye
Warp	Cotton	String				White	Natural
Weft	Cotton	String				White	Natural
	Wool	Commercial	Z	S	4	White	Natural
Bro-cading	Wool	Commercial	Z	S	4	Black	Aniline
	Wool	Commercial	Z	S	4	Green	Aniline
	Wool	Commercial	Z	S	4	Red	Aniline
	Wool	Commercial	Z	S	4	Dark blue	Aniline

30

Half of a Sash
68.46.46

Date: ca. 1950
Indefinite loan of Mr. Gilbert Maxwell

Hopi.
Warp faced weave with wrapped brocading and braided warp fringe.

Size: 99 cm. x 26.5 cm.
Count: 15 warps, 12 wefts.
Selvage: two cords; each 2-ply consisting of two pieces of 4-ply aniline dyed red commercial yarn.

	Fiber	*Type of Yarn*	*Spin*	*Twist*	*Ply*	*Color*	*Dye*
Warp	Cotton	String				White	Natural
Weft	Wool	Commercial	Z	S	4	Yellow	Aniline
Bro-cading	Wool	Commercial	Z	S	4	Red	Aniline
	Wool	Commercial	Z	S	4	Black	Aniline
	Wool	Commercial	Z	S	4	Green	Aniline
	Wool	Commercial	Z	S	4	Purple	Aniline

31

Fragment of a Sash
68.1.31

Date: ca. 1960
Donor unknown

Hopi.
Warp faced weave with wrapped brocading and warp fringe.

Size: 42 cm. x 18 cm.
Count: 14 warps, 9 wefts.
Selvage: one cord; natural white cotton string.

	Fiber	*Type of Yarn*	*Spin*	*Twist*	*Ply*	*Color*	*Dye*
Warp	Cotton	String				White	Natural
Weft	Cotton	String				White	Natural

Note: Cotton string in wefts is in two sizes.

32

Man's Wearing Blanket
63.34.141

Date: ca. 1930
Gift of Mr. and Mrs. Gilbert Maxwell

Hopi.
Diagonal twill weave.

Size: 107.5 cm. x 137 cm.
Selvage: two cords; 2-ply natural dark brown handspun. Ties
one quarter of the way down each side.

	Fiber	Type of Yarn	Spin	Twist	Ply	Color	Dye
Warp	Wool	Handspun	Z		1	White	Natural
	Wool	Handspun	Z		1	Dark brown	Natural
Weft	Wool	Handspun	Z		1	White	Natural
	Wool	Handspun	Z		1	Dark brown	Natural

33

Vest
64.18.22

Date: 1900–20
Gift of Mr. Maurice Maisel

Hopi.
Vest made from a cut-up sash. Knitted red wool panel under
each arm and the back is faced with green velvet.

Size: 45 cm. x 42 cm.

	Fiber	Type of Yarn	Spin	Twist	Ply	Color	Dye
Warp	Cotton	String				White	Natural
Weft	Cotton	String				White	Natural
Bro-cading	Wool	Commercial	Z	S	4	Green	Aniline
	Wool	Commercial	Z	S	4	Black	Aniline
	Wool	Commercial	Z	S	4	Red	Aniline
	Wool	Commercial	Z	S	4	Dark blue	Aniline

34

Shirt
69.55.1

Date: 1969
Gift of Mr. and Mrs. Bruce T. Ellis

San Juan.
Maria Ortiz, maker.
A copy of a Hopi type shirt. The design represents lightning, the fringes rain. Crocheted with commercial cotton yarn.

Size: 52.5 cm. x 40 cm. (across shoulders).

35

Leggings
63.34.189a, b

Date: ca. 1950
Gift of Mr. and Mrs. Gilbert Maxwell

Hopi?
Crocheted with 3-ply natural white commercial cotton yarn.

Size: 54.5 cm. x 18.5 cm.

36

Stockings
63.34.166

Date: ca. 1930
Gift of Mr. and Mrs. Gilbert Maxwell
Zuni?

Size: 36 cm. x 14.5 cm.

Knitted with dark blue aniline dyed
4-ply commercial wool yarn.

37

Stockings
67.33.4a, b

Date: ca. 1965
Purchase

Hopi?

Size: 35 cm. x 14.5 cm.

Knitted with black aniline dyed
4-ply commercial wool yarn.

38

Stockings
71.33.2

Date: 1971
Acquired from the Museum of Northern Arizona

Hopi, Hotevilla.
Sidney Namingha, maker.

Size: 33.5 cm. x 13 cm.

Knitted with black aniline
dyed 4-ply commercial wool yarn.

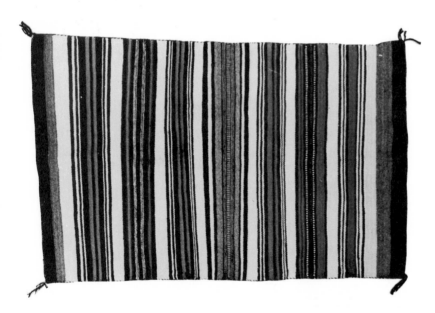

Miscellaneous

39

Saddle Blanket
63.34.156

Date: 1952
Gift of Mr. and Mrs. Gilbert Maxwell

Hopi, Moencopi.
Big Phillip, weaver.

Size: 150 cm. x 97 cm.
Count: 6 warps, 30 wefts.

Selvage: two cords; 2-ply natural dark brown handspun.

	Fiber	Type of Yarn	Spin	Twist	Ply	Color	Dye
Warp	Wool	Handspun	Z		1	White	Natural
Weft	Wool	Handspun	Z		1	White	Natural
	Wool	Handspun	Z		1	Black	Aniline
	Wool	Handspun	Z		1	Gray	Carded
	Wool	Handspun	Z		1	Dark blue	Aniline
	Wool	Handspun	Z		1	Light blue	Aniline
	Wool	Handspun	Z		1	Orange	Aniline

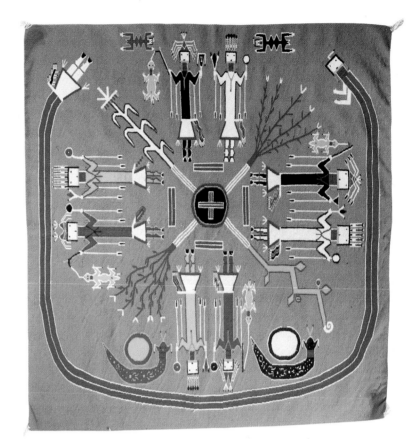

178.   Navajo rug, Sandpainting

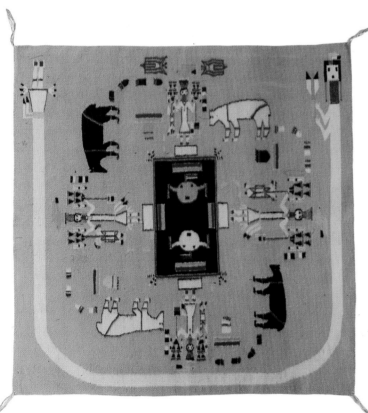

181.   Navajo rug, Sandpainting

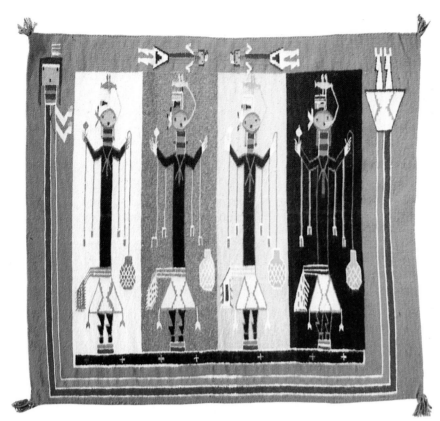

191. Navajo rug, Sandpainting

1. Pueblo manta

1. North Mexican serape

16. North Mexican blanket

24. North Mexican blanket

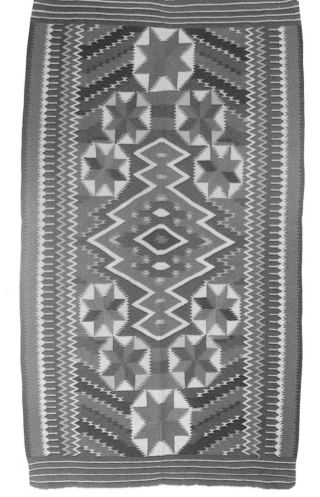

32. North Mexican blanket

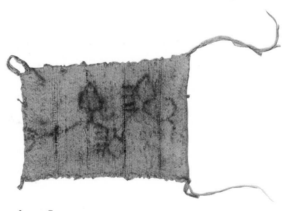

40

Rug/Blanket
69.67.21

Date: ca. 1960
Gift of Mr. and Mrs. Edwin L. Kennedy

Hopi.

Size: 183 cm. x 141.5 cm.
Count: 5 warps, 16 wefts.
Selvage: two cords; one 2-ply natural+ brown handspun, one
      2-ply natural white handspun.

	Fiber	Type of Yarn	Spin	Twist	Ply	Color	Dye
Warp	Cotton	String				White	Natural
Weft	Wool	Handspun	Z		1	White	Natural
	Wool	Handspun	Z		1	Black	Aniline
	Wool	Handspun	Z		1	Beige	Carded
	Wool	Handspun	Z		1	Yellow	Aniline
	Wool	Handspun	Z		1	Blue	Aniline

41

Pictorial Rug
55.20.51

Date: ca. 1900–20
Gift of Mrs. Richard Wetherill

Jemez.

This piece was given to Mrs. Wetherill's son by a Jemez man
who said it represented the Jemez watershed. It is supposedly
woven with fiber from the cottonwood tree and painted with
brown stain from puffballs.

Plain weave with painted design and remnants of feathers
(duck according to Mrs. Wetherill) woven into four rows about
7 cm. apart.

Size: 37 cm. x 26.5 cm.
Count: 12 warps, 8 wefts.
Selvage: two cords; 2-ply handspun cotton.

	Fiber	Type of Yarn	Spin	Twist	Ply	Color	Dye
Warp	Cotton	Handspun	Z	S	2	White	Natural
Weft	Cotton	Handspun	Z		1	White	Natural

The following group of sashes are commonly known as "rain sashes," as the long fringe flowing from the cotton covered squash blossom-like cornhusk ring is considered to represent rain falling from the clouds. These sashes were generally made by a complicated braiding technique (Underhill 1944:70–75). One of the Museum's pieces (no. 46) was woven on a loom as are most modern rain sashes.

42

Sash
55.20.6
Date: 1890–1920
Gift of Mrs. Richard Wetherill
Braided with 2-ply natural white handspun cotton.
Size: 131 cm. x 15.5 cm.

43

Sash
61.3.620
Date: 1900–20
Gift of Mrs. Joseph Imhof, the
Joseph Imhof Collection
Braided with 2-ply natural white handspun cotton.
Size: 131 cm. x 23.5 cm.

44

Sash
63.11.9

Date: 1920–60
Gift of Mr. and Mrs. Bruce T. Ellis
Braided with 2-ply natural white handspun cotton.
Size: 119 cm. x 10 cm.

45

Sash
75.1.257

Date: 1900–50
Donor unknown
Braided with 5-ply natural white commercial cotton yarn.
Size: 133 cm. x 19 cm.

46

Sash
76.1.39

Date: 1900–50
Donor unknown

Plain weave.

Size: 151 cm. x 20.5 cm.
Count: 14 warps, 24 wefts.
Selvage: three cords; 2-ply natural white cotton handspun.

	Fiber	Type of Yarn	Spin	Twist	Ply	Color	Dye
Warp	Cotton	Handspun	Z		1	White	Natural
Weft	Cotton	Handspun	Z		1	White	Natural

Note: Weft spun more tightly than warp.

47

Child's Belt
55.20.7

Date: ca. 1880
Gift of Mrs. Richard Wetherill

Hopi.
Given to Mrs. Wetherill when she visited a kachina dance as a girl.
Warp float weave.

Size: 125 cm. x 6 cm.
Count: 40 warps, 10 wefts.

	Fiber	Type of Yarn	Spin	Twist	Ply	Color	Dye
Warp	Wool	Commercial	Z	S	4	Olive green	Aniline
	Wool	Commercial	Z	S	4	Light green	Aniline
	Wool	Commercial	Z	S	4	Red	Aniline
	Wool	Commercial	Z	S	4	White	Natural
Weft	Wool	Commercial	Z	S	4	Brown	Aniline

48

Belt

61.3.483

Date: 1900–20

Gift of Mrs. Joseph Imhof, the
Joseph Imhof Collection

Warp float weave.

Size: 167 cm. x 8 cm.
Count: 36 warps, 12 wefts.

	Fiber	Type of Yarn	Spin	Twist	Ply	Color	Dye
Warp	Wool	Commercial	Z	S	4	Red	Aniline
	Wool	Commercial	Z	S	4	Green	Aniline
	Wool	Commercial	Z	S	4	Black	Aniline
Weft	Wool	Commercial	Z	S	4	Black	Aniline

49

Belt

61.3.484

Date: 1900–20

Gift of Mrs. Joseph Imhof, the
Joseph Imhof Collection

Warp float weave.

Size: 197 cm. x 9 cm.
Count: 40 warps, 11 wefts.

	Fiber	Type of Yarn	Spin	Twist	Ply	Color	Dye
Warp	Wool	Commercial	Z	S	4	Red	Aniline
	Wool	Commercial	Z	S	4	Green	Aniline
	Cotton	String				White	Natural
Weft	Cotton	String				White	Natural

50

Belt

61.3.482

Date: 1900–20
Gift of Mrs. Joseph Imhof, the
Joseph Imhof collection

Taos?
Warp float weave.

Size: 224.5 cm. x 6 cm.
Count: 44 warps, 12 wefts.

	Fiber	*Type of Yarn*	*Spin*	*Twist*	*Ply*	*Color*	*Dye*
Warp	Wool	Commercial	Z	S	4	Red	Aniline
	Wool	Commercial	Z	S	4	Green	Aniline
	Wool	Commercial	Z	S	4	Black	Aniline
Weft	Wool	Commercial	Z	S	4	Black	Aniline

51

Belt

61.3.485

Date: 1900–20
Gift of Mrs. Joseph Imhof, the
Joseph Imhof Collection

Taos?
Warp float weave.

Size: 63 cm. x 3.5 cm.
Count: 40 warps, 13 wefts.

	Fiber	*Type of Yarn*	*Spin*	*Twist*	*Ply*	*Color*	*Dye*
Warp	Wool	Commercial	Z	S	4	Red	Aniline
	Wool	Commercial	Z	S	4	Blue	Aniline
Weft	Cotton	String				White	Natural

52

Belt
61.3.486

Date: 1900–20
Gift of Mrs. Joseph Imhof, the
Joseph Imhof Collection

Taos?
Warp float weave.

Size: 236.5 cm. x 9 cm.
Count: 44 warps, 8 wefts.

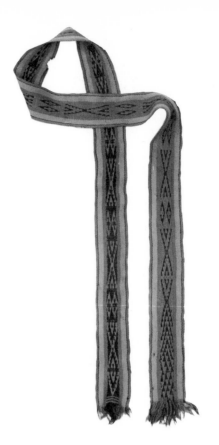

	Fiber	Type of Yarn	Spin	Twist	Ply	Color	Dye
Warp	Wool	Commercial	Z	S	4	Red	Aniline
	Wool	Commercial	Z	S	4	Black	Aniline
	Wool	Commercial	Z	S	4	Pale green	Aniline
	Wool	Commercial	Z	S	4	Faded brown	Aniline
Weft	Wool	Commercial	Z	S	4	Brown	Aniline

53

Belt
61.3.487

Date: 1900–20
Gift of Mrs. Joseph Imhof, the
Joseph Imhof Collection

Taos?
Warp float weave.

Size: 176 cm. x 6 cm.
Count: 40 warps, 16 wefts.

	Fiber	Type of Yarn	Spin	Twist	Ply	Color	Dye
Warp	Wool	Commercial	Z	S	4	Red	Aniline
	Wool	Commercial	Z	S	4	Black	Aniline
	Cotton	String				White	Natural
Weft	Cotton	String				White	Natural

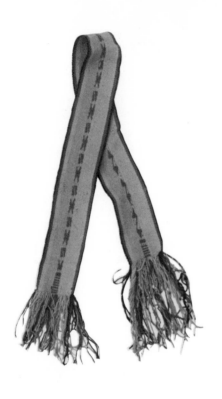

54

Belt
61.3.488
Date: 1900–20
Gift of Mrs. Joseph Imhof, the
Joseph Imhof Collection
Taos?
Warp float weave.

Size: 97 cm. x 7.5 cm.
Count: 30 warps, 13 wefts.

	Fiber	Type of Yarn	Spin	Twist	Ply	Color	Dye
Warp	Wool	Commercial	Z	S	4	Red	Aniline
	Wool	Commercial	Z	S	4	Green	Aniline
	Wool	Commercial	Z	S	4	Black	Aniline
Weft	Wool	Commercial	Z	S	4	Black	Aniline

55

Pair of Garters
74.28.22a, b
Date: 1900–20
Donor unknown
Hopi?
Warp float weave.

Size: 51.5 cm. x 3 cm. (a) and 40 cm. x 3 cm. (b).
Count: 36 warps, 15 wefts.

	Fiber	Type of Yarn	Spin	Twist	Ply	Color	Dye
Warp	Wool	Commercial	Z	S	4	Red	Aniline
	Wool	Commercial	Z	S	4	Blue/Green	Aniline
Weft	Cotton	String				White	Natural

56

Belt
61.2.5

Date: 1925
Gift of Mrs. Thomas Bush

Taos.
Warp float weave.

Size: 205 cm. x 10 cm.
Count: 36 warps, 13 wefts.

	Fiber	Type of Yarn	Spin	Twist	Ply	Color	Dye
Warp	Wool	Commercial	Z	S	4	Red	Aniline
	Wool	Commercial	Z	S	4	Green	Aniline
	Cotton	String				White	Natural
Weft	Cotton	String				White	Natural

57

Belt
73.30.24

Date: 1900–30
Transfer from Zimmerman Library,
University of New Mexico

Hopi?
Warp float weave.

Size: 90 cm. x 5 cm.
Count: 56 warps, 16 wefts.

	Fiber	Type of Yarn	Spin	Twist	Ply	Color	Dye
Warp	Wool	Commercial	Z	S	4	Red	Aniline
	Wool	Commercial	Z	S	4	Green	Aniline
	Cotton	String				White	Natural
Weft	Cotton	String				White	Natural

58

Belt
67.126.5

Date: 1950–60
Gift of Mr. and Mrs. Gilbert Maxwell

Hopi?
Warp float weave.

Size: 66 cm. x 5 cm.
Count: 68 warps, 20 wefts.

	Fiber	*Type of Yarn*	*Spin*	*Twist*	*Ply*	*Color*	*Dye*
Warp	Wool	Handspun	Z	S	2	Green	Aniline
	Wool	Handspun	Z	S	2	Red	Aniline
	Cotton	String				White	Natural
Weft	Cotton	String				White	Natural

59

Belt
63.34.187

Date: ca. 1950
Gift of Mr. and Mrs. Gilbert Maxwell

Warp float weave.

Size: 200 cm. (without fringe) x 9.5 cm.
Count: 40 warps, 12 wefts.

	Fiber	*Type of Yarn*	*Spin*	*Twist*	*Ply*	*Color*	*Dye*
Warp	Wool	Commercial	Z	S	4	Red	Aniline
	Wool	Commercial	Z	S	4	Green	Aniline
	Cotton	String				White	Natural
Weft	Cotton	String				White	Natural

60

Belt
71.33.4

Date: 1970–71
Acquired from the Museum of Northern Arizona

Hopi, Hotevilla.
Jack Pongyesvia, weaver.
Warp float weave.

Size: 212 cm. x 9 cm.
Count: 40 warps, 10 wefts.

	Fiber	Type of Yarn	Spin	Twist	Ply	Color	Dye
Warp	Wool	Commercial	Z	S	4	White	Natural
	Wool	Commercial	Z	S	4	Black	Aniline
	Wool	Commercial	Z	S	4	Red	Aniline
	Wool	Commercial	Z	S	4	Green	Aniline
	Wool	Commercial	Z	S	4	Yellow	Aniline
Weft	Wool	Commercial	Z	S	4	Blue	Aniline

3

NORTHERN MEXICO TEXTILES

The distinctive blanket patterns of the Saltillo region of northern Mexico influenced both Navajo and Rio Grande weaving. Saltillo wearing blankets, or serapes, are long and narrow, made in two pieces and sewn together with a slit left in the center for the head. The patterns usually have an elaborate central figure, either circular or diamond shaped, on a ground filled with small vertically arranged parallelograms, the whole surrounded by a narrow border. When worn, the central figure forms a collar covering the shoulders and upper body. Saltillo region weavers may have come directly from Spain bringing the design system with them in its fully developed form. The basic pattern may derive from a Persian rug style originating in the Sarouk area (Boyd 1973: personal communication).

The Museum's series of Saltillo area serapes ranges from early cochineal and indigo dyed specimens of the eighteenth century, through the aniline dyed ones of the late nineteenth century until about 1915 when the style was replaced by textiles with nationalistic motifs such as Aztec calendar stones.

The Museum owns only four pieces of Indian weaving from northern Mexico. Even less is known and written about the indigenous weaving than about the Saltillo tradition. The blankets tend to be coarse utilitarian items.

1

Serape
63.34.87

Date: eighteenth century?
Gift of Mr. and Mrs. Gilbert Maxwell

Saltillo.
Woven in two pieces and sewn down the center.

Size: 233.5 cm. x 127.5 cm.
Count: 23 warps, 96 wefts.
Edge Finish: warp, completely stitched over; weft, over one
warp.

See plate section.

	Fiber	Type of Yarn	Spin	Twist	Ply	Color	Dye
Warp	Linen	Handspun	Z	S	2	Beige	Natural
Weft	Wool	Handspun	Z		1	White	Natural
	Wool	Handspun	Z		1	Dark blue	Indigo
	Wool	Handspun	Z		1	Light blue	Indigo
	Wool	Handspun	Z		1	Red	Cochineal
	Wool	Handspun	Z		1	Pink	Cochineal
	Wool	Handspun	Z		1	Purple	Cochineal
	Wool	Handspun	Z		1	Yellow	Natural
	Wool	Handspun	Z		1	Green	Indigo & yellow

2

Serape
63.34.89

Date: eighteenth century
Gift of Mr. and Mrs. Gilbert Maxwell

Saltillo.
Woven in two pieces and sewn down the center.

Size: 241 cm. x 151 cm.
Count: 22 warps, 84 wefts.
Edge Finish: warp, missing; weft, last two warps are paired.

	Fiber	Type of Yarn	Spin	Twist	Ply	Color	Dye
Warp	Linen	Handspun	Z	S	2	White	Natural
Weft	Wool	Handspun	Z		1	White	Natural
	Wool	Handspun	Z		1	Dark blue	Indigo
	Wool	Handspun	Z		1	Light blue	Indigo
	Wool	Handspun	Z		1	Gold	Vegetal

3

Serape
70.65.1

Date: 1800–50
Gift of Dr. Scott Adler

Formerly in Maxwell Collection.
Woven in two pieces and sewn together.

Size: 241 cm. x 123 cm.
Count: 12 warps, 60 wefts.
Edge Finish: warp, completely stitched under; weft, completely stitched under.

	Fiber	Type of Yarn	Spin	Twist	Ply	Color	Dye
Warp	Linen	Handspun	Z	S	2	White	Natural
Weft	Wool	Handspun	Z		1	White	Natural
	Wool	Handspun	Z		1	Black	Natural+
	Wool	Handspun	Z		1	Red	Cochineal
	Wool	Handspun	Z		1	Pink	Cochineal
	Wool	Handspun	Z		1	Gold	Vegetal
	Wool	Handspun	Z		1	Blue	Indigo
	Wool	Handspun	Z		1	Green	Indigo & yellow

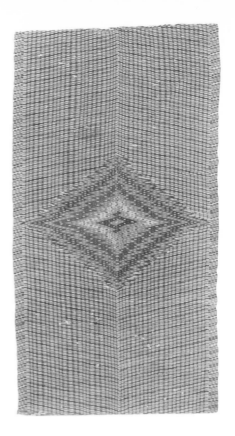

4

Serape
63.34.157

Date: 1800–50
Gift of Mr. and Mrs. Gilbert Maxwell

Saltillo.
Woven in two pieces and sewn down the center.

Size: 253.5 cm. x 126 cm.
Count: 14 warps, 60 wefts.
Edge Finish: warp, a knotted chain; weft, last two warps paired.

	Fiber	Type of Yarn	Spin	Twist	Ply	Color	Dye
Warp	Wool	Handspun	Z	S	2	White	Natural
Weft	Wool	Handspun	Z		1	Black	Natural+
	Wool	Handspun	Z		1	Rose	Cochineal
	Wool	Handspun	Z		1	Pink	Cochineal
	Wool	Handspun	Z		1	Purple	Cochineal
	Wool	Handspun	Z		1	Blue	Indigo
	Wool	Handspun	Z		1	Yellow	Vegetal
	Wool	Handspun	Z		1	Green	Indigo & yellow

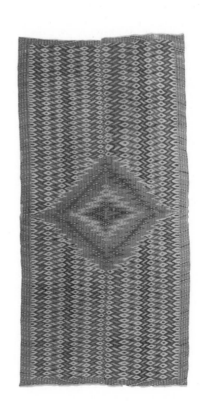

5

Serape
63.34.88

Date: 1800–50
Gift of Mr. and Mrs. Gilbert Maxwell
Saltillo.
Woven in two pieces and sewn down the center.
On either side of the central diamond are a pair of sheep with baskets in their mouths.
Size: 235 cm. x 131 cm.
Count: 22 warps, 104 wefts.
Edge Finish: warp, netted together in complex pattern; weft, last three warps are paired.

	Fiber	Type of Yarn	Spin	Twist	Ply	Color	Dye
Warp	Linen	Handspun	Z	S	2	White	Natural
Weft	Wool	Handspun	Z		1	White	Natural
	Wool	Handspun	Z		1	Black	Natural+
	Wool	Handspun	Z		1	Blue	Indigo
	Wool	Handspun	Z		1	Red	Cochineal
	Wool	Handspun	Z		1	Pink	Cochineal
	Wool	Handspun	Z		1	Gold	Vegetal

6

Serape
63.34.163

Date: 1870–1900
Gift of Mr. and Mrs. Gilbert Maxwell
Saltillo.
Woven in two pieces and sewn down the center.
Size: 190 cm. x 110 cm.
Count: 12 warps, 30 wefts.
Edge Finish: warp, six warps knotted together forming a net fringe; weft, last two warps paired.

	Fiber	Type of Yarn	Spin	Twist	Ply	Color	Dye
Warp	Cotton	String				White	Natural
Weft	Wool	Handspun	Z		1	White	Natural
	Wool	Handspun	Z		1	Black	Aniline
	Wool	Handspun	Z		1	Gray	Aniline
	Wool	Handspun	Z		1	Purple	Aniline
	Wool	Handspun	Z		1	Red	Aniline
	Wool	Handspun	Z		1	Blue	Aniline
	Wool	Handspun	Z		1	Orange	Aniline

7

Serape
63.34.161

Date: 1880–1900
Gift of Mr. and Mrs. Gilbert Maxwell

Saltillo.
Woven in two pieces and sewn down the center.

Size: 216.5 cm. x 116 cm.
Count: 14 warps, 56 wefts.
Edge Finish: warp, tied together in groups of four, long
           knotted fringe; weft, last two warps paired.

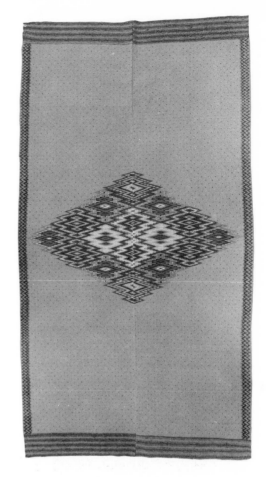

	Fiber	Type of Yarn	Spin	Twist	Ply	Color	Dye
Warp	Linen	Handspun	Z	S	2	Beige	Natural
Weft	Wool	Handspun	Z		1	Red	Aniline
	Wool	Handspun	Z		1	Black	Aniline
	Wool	Handspun	Z		1	Maroon	Aniline
	Wool	Handspun	Z		1	Yellow	Aniline
	Wool	Handspun	Z		1	Orange	Aniline
	Wool	Handspun	Z		1	Green	Aniline
	Wool	Handspun	Z		1	White	Natural
	Wool	Handspun	Z		1	Purple	Aniline
	Wool	Handspun	Z		1	Dark blue	Aniline
	Wool	Handspun	Z		1	Light blue	Aniline
	Wool	Handspun	Z		1	Lavender	Aniline

8

Serape
63.34.164

Date: ca. 1915
Gift of Mr. and Mrs. Gilbert Maxwell

Saltillo.
Woven in two pieces and sewn together.

Size: 217.5 cm. x 195 cm.   Count: 24 warps, 72 wefts.
Edge Finish: warp, stitched under with a sewing machine;
           weft, last warp paired.

	Fiber	Type of Yarn	Spin	Twist	Ply	Color	Dye
Warp	Wool	Handspun	Z	S	2	White	Natural
Weft	Wool	Handspun	Z		1	White	Natural
	Wool	Handspun	Z		1	Black	Aniline
	Wool	Handspun	Z		1	Red	Aniline
	Wool	Handspun	Z		1	Green (6 shades)	Aniline
	Wool	Handspun	Z		1	Blue (6 shades)	Aniline
	Wool	Handspun	Z		1	Red (6 shades)	Aniline
	Wool	Handspun	Z		1	Yellow (5 shades)	Aniline
	Silk	Handspun	Z		1	White	Natural

9

Rug or Table Throw
68.101.8

Date: ca. 1950
Gift of Mrs. Elaine Hudson

Northern Mexico. Size: 118 cm. x 58 cm.
Woven in one piece. Count: 20 warps, 50 wefts.

Edge Finish: warp, ten warps twisted together; weft, last warp consists of twelve strings.

	Fiber	Type of Yarn	Spin	Twist	Ply	Color	Dye
Warp	Cotton	String				White	Natural
Weft	Cotton	String				White	Natural
	Wool	Handspun	Z		1	White	Natural
	Wool	Handspun	Z		1	Black	Aniline
	Wool	Handspun	Z		1	Red (6 shades)	Aniline
	Wool	Handspun	Z		1	Blue (5 shades)	Aniline
	Wool	Handspun	Z		1	Pink (4 shades)	Aniline
	Wool	Handspun	Z		1	Green (6 shades)	Aniline
	Wool	Handspun	Z		1	Brown (3 shades)	Aniline

10

Rug or Table Throw
68.101.7

Date: ca. 1950
Gift of Mrs. Elaine Hudson

Northern Mexico. Size: 119 cm. x 57 cm.
Woven in one piece. Count: 20 warps, 64 wefts.

Edge Finish: warp, eight warps tied together; weft, last warp consists of ten strings.

	Fiber	Type of Yarn	Spin	Twist	Ply	Color	Dye
Warp	Cotton	String	Z	S	2	White	Natural
Weft	Cotton	String	Z	S	4	White	Natural
	Wool	Handspun	Z		1	Brown	Aniline
	Wool	Handspun	Z		1	Orange	Aniline
	Wool	Handspun	Z		1	Maroon	Aniline
	Wool	Handspun	Z		1	Red	Aniline
	Wool	Handspun	Z		1	Pink (3 shades)	Aniline
	Wool	Handspun	Z		1	Blue (4 shades)	Aniline
	Wool	Handspun	Z		1	Green (2 shades)	Aniline
	Wool	Handspun	Z		1	Yellow	Aniline
	Wool	Handspun	Z		1	Chartreuse	Aniline

11

Blanket
63.34.154

Date: ca. 1935

Gift of Mr. and Mrs. Gilbert Maxwell

Tarahumara.

Size: 223 cm. x 116 cm.
Count: 5 warps, 16 wefts.
Edge Finish: warp, continuous and held by 2-ply natural white
              handspun cord.

	Fiber	Type of Yarn	Spin	Twist	Ply	Color	Dye
Warp	Wool	Handspun	Z	S	2	White &	Natural
						brown plied	
Weft	Wool	Handspun	Z		1	White	Natural
	Wool	Handspun	Z		1	Brown	Natural

12

Blanket
63.34.155

Date: ca. 1938

Gift of Mr. and Mrs. Gilbert Maxwell

Tarahumara.

Purchased in 1938 in Cuschcuriachick.

Size: 178 cm. x 137 cm.
Count: 7 warps, 20 wefts.
Edge Finish: warp, tied in pairs.

	Fiber	Type of Yarn	Spin	Twist	Ply	Color	Dye
Warp	Wool	Handspun	Z		1	Brown	Natural
Weft	Wool	Handspun	Z		1	Brown	Natural
	Wool	Handspun	Z		1	White	Natural
	Wool	Handspun	Z		1	Gold	Vegetal

13

Blanket
66.80.1

Date: ca. 1950

Anonymous gift in honor of Dr. W. W. Hill

Tarahumara.

Size: 208 cm. x 96.5 cm.
Count: 5 warps, 14 wefts.
Edge Finish: warp, pairs twisted together and two of these
　　　　　　pairs twisted and knotted together.

	Fiber	Type of Yarn	Spin	Twist	Ply	Color	Dye
Warp	Wool	Handspun	Z		1	Dark brown	Natural
Weft	Wool	Handspun	Z		1	White	Natural
	Wool	Handspun	Z		1	Med. brown	Natural

14

Blanket
69.2.1

Date: 1930–60

Gift of Dr. W. W. Hill

Yaqui-Mayo.

Size: 211 cm. x 111 cm.
Count: 7 warps, 30 wefts.
Edge Finish: warp, three warps tied together; weft, no cord,
　　　　　　over one warp.

	Fiber	Type of Yarn	Spin	Twist	Ply	Color	Dye
Warp	Wool	Handspun	Z		1	White	Natural
Weft	Wool	Handspun	Z		1	White	Natural
	Wool	Handspun	Z		1	Dark brown	Natural+
	Wool	Handspun	Z		1	Med. brown	Natural
	Wool	Handspun	Z		1	Beige	Carded
	Wool	Handspun	Z		1	Gold	Vegetal (?)
	Wool	Handspun	Z		1	Med. blue	Aniline
	Wool	Handspun	Z		1	Light blue	Aniline

4
RIO GRANDE TEXTILES

Weaving done by the Spanish settlers of New Mexico and southern Colorado is commonly called "Rio Grande," because most was made at villages located along the drainage system of that river. The earliest Spanish settlers probably did not bring heavy looms with them, but rather the knowledge of how to build and use them. The combined production of both Indian and Spanish looms soon made textiles one of the province's chief exports.

The horizontal European loom used by the Spaniards is quite different from that used by Pueblo and Navajo weavers. The latter can be disassembled quite easily and carried anywhere and has simple stick heddles tied to the warps. The Spanish loom is a permanent installation with fixed heddles operated by a foot mechanism. Differences in manufacturing techniques based upon the construction of the loom can be used to distinguish Navajo or Pueblo from Rio Grande weaving. The Spanish loom can accommodate many yards of warp and as the weaving progresses the cloth is rolled on a beam. When all the warp on a loom is used the cloth is taken off, unrolled, and cut into individual pieces across the warps. The cutting leaves a fringe of warps that must be secured by being knotted together. The Navajo and Pueblo warps are continuous, being wound back and forth within the textile, producing a finished edge along the top and bottom as well as the sides. The texture of Rio Grande textiles is different also, due to the low proportion of thick 2-ply warp elements and high proportion of loosely spun wefts.

The Rio Grande loom was narrow but textiles wider than the loom were produced in either of two ways. Two identical pieces could be sewn together longitudinally but the patterns then frequently did not exactly match. Alternatively the loom could be warped. Weaving was then begun from left to right, and when the right edge was reached, the weft was passed around, under, and woven back to the left. This process always left at least one doubled warp in the center and the full width was not seen until the textile was taken off the loom. In the 1890s a wider loom was introduced at the village of Chimayo by the Santa Fe trader J. S. Candelario, thus simplifying the weaving of wider textiles (Mrs. Richard Wetherill n.d.: unpublished journal).

Many of the dyes used by the Navajo and Pueblo weavers were also used by the Rio Grande Spanish. Indigo was imported from the south, and rabbit brush and mountain mahogany (called logwood) were found locally. Rio Grande weavers also used aniline dyes and commercial yarns when they became available. A few examples of cochineal dye used on handspun wool are evidence that the Spanish-American weavers had access to this dye that seems not to have been available to Navajo or Pueblo weavers except by unraveling industrially made cloth or in the form of commercial yarn.

The history of Rio Grande weaving is not well documented. Most of the Museum's Rio Grande textiles are dated as the Navajo ones are by the presence of certain yarns and dyes; however, further research may date them earlier than the nineteenth century.

The term "Chimayo" is often applied to Rio Grande textiles in much the same way as "Hopi" is used as a name for Pueblo textiles, and for the same reasons. Both communities kept old weaving traditions going long after they had been abandoned in other towns. Chimayo has an active weaving industry to this day, but textiles labeled Chimayo are not always made there.

15

Blanket
63.34.77

Date: 1850–70
Gift of Mr. and Mrs. Gilbert Maxwell

Rio Grande.
Woven in one piece, two paired warps in the center.

Size: 237 cm. x 130 cm.
Count: 7 warps, 32 wefts.
Edge Finish: warp, knotted chain; weft, one set of warps paired and twisted.

	Fiber	Type of Yarn	Spin	Twist	Ply	Color	Dye
Warp	Wool	Handspun	Z	S	2	White	Natural
Weft	Wool	Handspun	Z		1	White	Natural
	Wool	Handspun	Z		1	Brown	Natural
	Wool	Handspun	Z		1	Blue	Indigo

16

Blanket
63.34.76

Date: 1850–70
Gift of Mr. and Mrs. Gilbert Maxwell

Rio Grande.
In Pedro Muniz Collection before 1902.
Woven in two pieces and sewn together.

See plate section.

Size: 218 cm. x 134.5 cm.
Count: 5 warps, 28 wefts.
Edge Finish: warp, repaired by a Navajo weaver with a cord
           and tassels added; weft, last two warps paired.

	Fiber	Type of Yarn	Spin	Twist	Ply	Color	Dye
Warp	Wool	Handspun	Z	S	2	White	Natural
Weft	Wool	Handspun	Z		1	White	Natural
	Wool	Handspun	Z		1	Brown	Natural
	Wool	Handspun	Z		1	Blue	Indigo

17

Rug Fragment
74.28.23

Date: 1860–80
Donor unknown

Rio Grande.

Size: 51 cm. x 56 cm.
Count: 6 warps, 18 wefts.
Edge Finish: warp, missing; weft, last warp paired.

	Fiber	Type of Yarn	Spin	Twist	Ply	Color	Dye
Warp	Wool	Handspun	Z	S	2	White	Natural
Weft	Wool	Handspun	Z		1	White	Natural
	Wool	Handspun	Z		1	Brown	Natural
	Wool	Handspun	Z		1	Med. blue	Indigo

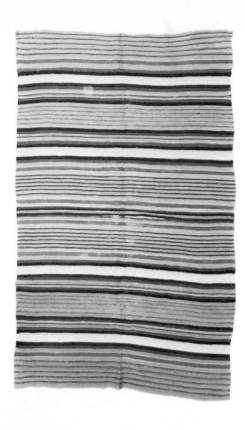

18

Blanket
65.42.152

Date: ca. 1850–70
Transfer from Zimmerman Library,
University of New Mexico

Rio Grande.
Woven in one piece with a group of four warps in the center.

Size: 213.5 cm. x 130 cm.
Count: 6 warps, 36 wefts.
Edge Finish: warp, knotted chain; weft, last four warps paired.

	Fiber	Type of Yarn	Spin	Twist	Ply	Color	Dye
Warp	Wool	Handspun	Z	S	2	White	Natural
Weft	Wool	Handspun	Z		1	White	Natural
	Wool	Handspun	Z		1	Brown	Natural
	Wool	Handspun	Z		1	Gold	Vegetal
	Wool	Handspun	Z		1	Yellow	Vegetal
	Wool	Handspun	Z		1	Blue	Indigo
	Wool	Handspun	Z		1	Blue/Green	Indigo & yellow

19

Blanket
65.42.154

Date: 1850–70
Transfer from Zimmerman Library,
University of New Mexico

Rio Grande.
Woven in one piece, six warps in the center are paired.

Size: 243 cm. x 134 cm.
Count: 5 warps, 30 wefts.
Edge Finish: warp, all damaged and stitched under; weft, last
two warps paired.

	Fiber	Type of Yarn	Spin	Twist	Ply	Color	Dye
Warp	Wool	Handspun	Z	S	2	White	Natural
Weft	Wool	Handspun	Z		1	White	Natural
	Wool	Handspun	Z		1	Brown	Natural
	Wool	Handspun	Z		1	Gold	Vegetal
	Wool	Handspun	Z		1	Yellow	Vegetal

20

Blanket
63.34.81

Date: 1850–70
Gift of Mr. and Mrs. Gilbert Maxwell

Rio Grande.
Purchased from Fred Harvey Company in 1945. Formerly in
J. F. Huckle Collection.
Woven in one piece, two paired warps in center.

Size: 235 cm. x 124 cm.
Count: 6 warps, 34 wefts.
Edge Finish: warp, knotted chain; weft, last warp paired and
twisted.

	Fiber	Type of Yarn	Spin	Twist	Ply	Color	Dye
Warp	Wool	Handspun	Z	S	2	White	Natural
Weft	Wool	Handspun	Z		1	White	Natural
	Wool	Handspun	Z		1	Brown	Natural
	Wool	Handspun	Z		1	Blue	Indigo
	Wool	Handspun	Z		1	Yellow	Vegetal
	Wool	Handspun	Z		1	Gold	Logwood
	Wool	Handspun	Z		1	Green	Indigo & yellow

21

Blanket
65.42.153

Date: 1850–60
Transfer from Zimmerman Library,
University of New Mexico

Rio Grande.
Woven in one piece, four warps paired in the center.

Size: 233 cm. x 117 cm.
Count: 5 warps, 36 wefts.
Edge Finish: warp, three warps tied together; weft, last two
warps paired.

	Fiber	Type of Yarn	Spin	Twist	Ply	Color	Dye
Warp	Wool	Handspun	Z	S	2	White	Natural
Weft	Wool	Handspun	Z		1	White	Natural
	Wool	Handspun	Z		1	Brown	Natural
	Wool	Handspun	Z		1	Blue	Indigo
	Wool	Handspun	Z		1	Gold	Mormon tea (?)
	Wool	Handspun	Z		1	Yellow	Rabbit brush
	Wool	Handspun	Z		1	Green	Indigo & yellow

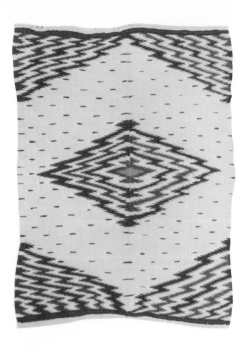

22

Blanket
63.34.84

Date: ca. 1850
Gift of Mr. and Mrs. Gilbert Maxwell

Rio Grande.
Formerly in the Jim Seligman Collection.
Woven in two pieces and sewn down the center.

Size: 189 cm. x 134 cm.
Count: 5 warps, 40 wefts.
Edge Finish: warp, knotted chain; weft, last warp paired.

	Fiber	Type of Yarn	Spin	Twist	Ply	Color	Dye
Warp	Wool	Handspun	Z	S	2	White	Natural
Weft	Wool	Handspun	Z		1	White	Natural
	Wool	Handspun	Z		1	Brown	Natural
	Wool	Handspun	Z		1	Blue	Indigo
	Wool	Commercial	Z	S	3	Pink	Cochineal

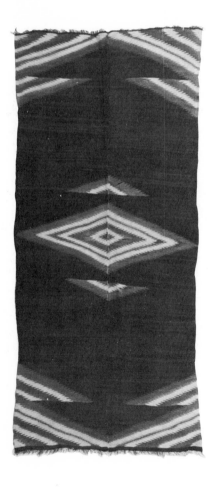

23

Blanket
63.34.79

Date: ca. 1850
Gift of Mr. and Mrs. Gilbert Maxwell

Rio Grande.
Woven in two pieces and sewn down the center.

Size: 213 cm. x 95.5 cm.
Count: 8 warps, 36 wefts (handspun) and 8 warps, 46 wefts (commercial yarn).
Edge Finish: warp, pairs of warps tied together; weft, last two warps twisted together.

	Fiber	Type of Yarn	Spin	Twist	Ply	Color	Dye
Warp	Wool	Handspun	Z	S	2	Beige	Carded
Weft	Wool	Handspun	Z		1	Brown	Natural
	Wool	Handspun	Z		1	White	Natural
	Wool	Handspun	Z		1	Blue	Indigo
	Wool	Commercial	Z	S	3	Red	Cochineal

24

Blanket
63.34.82

Date: 1850–70
Gift of Mr. and Mrs. Gilbert Maxwell

Rio Grande.
Woven in two pieces and sewn down the center.

Size: 224 cm. x 142 cm.
Count: 6 warps, 28 wefts.
Edge Finish: warp, pairs of warps tied together; weft, last four
  warps are paired.

	Fiber	Type of Yarn	Spin	Twist	Ply	Color	Dye
Warp	Wool	Handspun	Z	S	2	White	Natural
	Wool	Handspun	Z	S	2	Brown	Natural
Weft	Wool	Handspun	Z		1	White	Natural
	Wool	Handspun	Z		1	Gold	Vegetal
	Wool	Handspun	Z		1	Blue	Indigo
						(2 shades)	

See plate section.

25

Blanket
63.34.85

Date: 1850–70
Gift of Mr. and Mrs. Gilbert Maxwell
Formerly in J. Lorenzo Hubbell Collection.

Rio Grande.
Woven in one piece, warp paired in center.

Size: 167 cm. x 117.5 cm.
Count: 6 warps, 36 wefts.
Edge Finish: both warp and weft cords added by a Navajo
  reweaver. The discontinuous warp is tucked back
  into the blanket. The unusual design motifs were
  also added by the reweaver. Previously called a
  "slave blanket" because of this combination of
  Mexican pattern with Navajo technique.

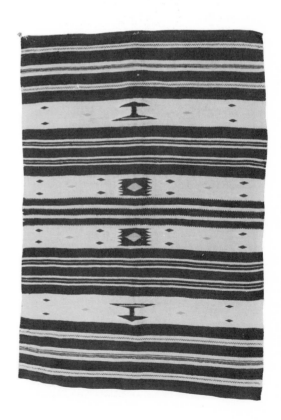

	Fiber	Type of Yarn	Spin	Twist	Ply	Color	Dye
Warp	Wool	Handspun	Z	S	2	White	Natural
Weft	Wool	Handspun	Z		1	White	Natural
	Wool	Handspun	Z		1	Brown	Natural
	Wool	Handspun	Z		1	Dark blue	Indigo
	Wool	Handspun	Z		1	Med. blue	Aniline
	Wool	Handspun	Z		1	Pink	Aniline
						(faded red)	

26

Blanket
63.34.83

Date: 1865–75
Gift of Mr. and Mrs. Gilbert Maxwell

Rio Grande.
Design is based on the Saltillo serape.
Woven in two pieces and sewn down the center.

Size: 212 cm. x 122 cm.
Count: 7 warps, 30 wefts.
Edge Finish: warp, repaired by a Navajo with a cord weft; last three warps are paired.

	Fiber	Type of Yarn	Spin	Twist	Ply	Color	Dye
Warp	Wool and goat hair	Handspun	Z	S	2	White	Natural
Weft	Wool and goat hair	Handspun	Z		1	White	Natural
	Wool and goat hair	Handspun	Z		1	Black	Natural+
	Wool and goat hair	Handspun	Z		1	Blue	Indigo
	Wool	Commercial	Z	S	3	Red	Cochineal
	Wool	Commercial	Z	S	3	Green	Aniline (?)
	Wool	Commercial	Z	S	2	Faded Purple/ Blue	Aniline
	Wool	Commercial	Z	S	3	Gold	Aniline
	Wool	Commercial	Z	S	3	Gray	Aniline
	Wool	Commercial	Z	S	3	Red/Green	Aniline

Note: The commercial green, purple/blue, red/green, and gray yarns are all used in pairs.

27

Blanket
63.34.80

Date: 1880–1900
Gift of Mr. and Mrs. Gilbert Maxwell

Rio Grande.
Woven in two pieces and sewn down the center.

Size: 178 cm. x 123 cm.
Count: 6 warps, 32 wefts.
Edge Finish: warp, knotted chain; weft, last warp paired.

	Fiber	Type of Yarn	Spin	Twist	Ply	Color	Dye
Warp	Cotton	String				White	Natural
Weft	Wool	Handspun	Z	S	2	Brown	Natural
	Wool	Handspun	Z	S	2	Purple	Aniline
	Wool	Handspun	Z	S	2	Yellow	Aniline

Note: A mottled effect is created by weaving 2-ply strands of several colors together but without plying them.

28

Blanket
71.35.1

Date: 1880–1900
Gift of Miss Lillian Colish

Rio Grande.
Woven in one piece, warp paired in center.

Size: 210 cm. x 121.5 cm.
Count: 6 warps, 24 wefts.
Edge Finish: warp, four warps tied together; weft, last three
      warps are paired.

	Fiber	Type of Yarn	Spin	Twist	Ply	Color	Dye
Warp	Cotton	String				White	Natural
Weft	Wool	Handspun	Z		1	Red	Aniline
	Wool	Handspun	Z		1	Blue	Aniline
	Wool	Handspun	Z		1	Pink	Aniline
	Wool	Handspun	Z		1	Lavender (faded purple)	Aniline

29

Blanket
63.34.103

Date: 1890–1900
Gift of Mr. and Mrs. Gilbert Maxwell

Rio Grande.
Woven in one piece.

Size: 227.5 cm. x 110 cm.
Count: 6 warps, 24 wefts.
Edge Finish: warp, knotted chain; weft, last three warps are
      thicker.

	Fiber	Type of Yarn	Spin	Twist	Ply	Color	Dye
Warp	Wool	Handspun	Z	S	2	White	Natural
	Wool	Handspun	Z	S	2	Brown	Natural
Weft	Wool	Handspun	Z		1	White	Natural
	Wool	Handspun	Z		1	Brown	Natural
	Wool	Handspun	Z		1	Blue	Indigo
	Wool	Handspun	Z		1	Orange	Aniline
	Wool	Handspun	Z		1	Lavender	Aniline
	Wool	Handspun	Z		1	Pale yellow	Aniline

30

Blanket
63.34.98

Date: 1880–90
Gift of Mr. and Mrs. Gilbert Maxwell

Rio Grande.
Woven in one piece.

Size: 228 cm. x 138 cm.
Count: 5 warps, 20 wefts.
Edge Finish: warp, knotted chain; weft, last warp paired.

	Fiber	Type of Yarn	Spin	Twist	Ply	Color	Dye
Warp	Wool	Handspun	Z	S	2	White	Natural
Weft	Wool	Handspun	Z		1	White	Natural
	Wool	Handspun	Z		1	Red	Aniline
	Wool	Handspun	Z		1	Black	Aniline
	Wool	Handspun	Z		1	Orange	Aniline
	Wool	Handspun	Z		1	Green (faded)	Aniline

31

Rug
71.39.1

Date: ca. 1900
Transfer from the Office of the Dean of the
College of Arts and Sciences,
University of New Mexico

Rio Grande.
Woven in one piece, one set of paired warps in center.

Size: 330 cm. x 200 cm.
Count: 5 warps, 36 wefts.
Edge Finish: warp, three warps tied together; weft, over a
    single warp.

	Fiber	Type of Yarn	Spin	Twist	Ply	Color	Dye
Warp	Wool	Handspun	S	Z	2	White	Natural
Weft	Wool	Handspun	S		1	White	Natural
	Wool	Handspun	S		1	Turquoise (faded)	Aniline
	Wool	Handspun	Z		1	Turquoise (faded)	Aniline

32

Blanket
63.34.107

Date: 1890–1900
Gift of Mr. and Mrs. Gilbert Maxwell

Rio Grande, El Valle.
This pattern, called "Vallero," was originated by Patricia Montoya (see Boyd 1974).
Registered with the Laboratory of Anthropology, Santa Fe, no. 635.
Woven in two pieces and sewn down the center.

Size: 192.5 cm. x 109.5 cm.
Count: 9 warps, 30 wefts.
Edge Finish: warp, three warps tied together; weft, last warp paired.

	Fiber	*Type of Yarn*	*Spin*	*Twist*	*Ply*	*Color*	*Dye*
Warp	Cotton	String	Z	S	3	White	Natural
Weft	Wool	Commercial	Z	S	4	Red/Purple	Aniline
	Wool	Commercial	Z	S	4	Red	Aniline
	Wool	Commercial	Z	S	4	Orange	Aniline
	Wool	Commercial	Z	S	4	Purple	Aniline
	Wool	Commercial	Z	S	4	Yellow	Aniline
	Wool	Commercial	Z	S	4	Turquoise	Aniline
	Wool	Commercial	Z	S	4	Black	Aniline
	Wool	Commercial	Z	S	4	White	Aniline

33

Serape
55.20.68a, b

Date: ca. 1900
Gift of Mrs. Richard Wetherill
Woven in two pieces and sewn down the center, but the pieces have been separated.

Size: 180.5 cm. x 47 cm.
Count: 18 warps, 30 wefts.
Edge Finish: completely sewn over.

	Fiber	*Type of Yarn*	*Spin*	*Twist*	*Ply*	*Color*	*Dye*
Warp	Cotton	String	Z	S	2	White	Natural
Weft	Wool	Handspun	Z		1	White	Natural
	Wool	Handspun	Z		1	Red	Aniline
	Wool	Handspun	Z		1	Gray	Aniline
	Wool	Handspun	Z		1	Brown	Natural

See plate section.

34, 35

Pair of Serapes
55.20.46 and 55.20.47

Date: ca. 1895
Gift of Mrs. Richard Wetherill

Possibly Mexican.
Given to the Wetherills as a wedding present in 1896 by J. S. Candelario.
Woven in one piece.

Size: 205 cm. x 101 cm.
Count: 14 warps, 64 wefts.
Edge Finish: warp, four warps tied together; weft, last two warps are paired.

	Fiber	Type of Yarn	Spin	Twist	Ply	Color	Dye
Warp	Wool	Handspun	Z		1	White	Natural
Weft	Wool	Handspun	Z		1	White	Natural
	Wool	Handspun	Z		1	Black	Aniline
	Wool	Handspun	Z		1	Gray	Aniline
	Wool	Handspun	Z		1	Red	Aniline
	Wool	Handspun	Z		1	Purple	Aniline
	Wool	Handspun	Z		1	Light green	Aniline
	Wool	Handspun	Z		1	Peach	Aniline
A series of variegated yarns							
	Wool	Commercial	Z	S	4	Pinks	Aniline
	Wool	Commercial	Z	S	4	Blue to green to yellow	Aniline
	Wool	Commercial	Z	S	4	Purple to lavender	Aniline
	Wool	Commercial	Z	S	4	Rust brown to yellow	Aniline
	Wool	Commercial	Z	S	4	Maroon to pink	Aniline
	Wool	Commercial	Z	S	4	Blues	Aniline

36

Rug or Chair Throw
55.20.45

Date: ca. 1890
Gift of Mrs. Richard Wetherill

Rio Grande, Chimayo.
Owned by Richard Wetherill at time of his marriage in 1896.
Woven in one piece.

Size: 129 cm. x 55.5 cm.
Count: 13 warps, 50 wefts.
Edge Finish: warp, completely missing; weft, last warp consists
                    of six strands.

	Fiber	Type of Yarn	Spin	Twist	Ply	Color	Dye
Warp	Wool	Handspun	Z	S	2	Blue	Aniline
Weft	Wool	Handspun	Z		1	White	Natural
	Wool	Handspun	Z		1	Red	Aniline
	Wool	Handspun	Z		1	Blue	Aniline
	Wool	Handspun	Z		1	Pink	Aniline
	Wool	Handspun	Z		1	Gray	Aniline

37

Serape
55.20.48a, b

Date: ca. 1896
Gift of Mrs. Richard Wetherill

Rio Grande, Chimayo.
Woven in two pieces and originally sewn down the center,
but separated for many years.
Given as a wedding gift soon after 1896 by J. S. Candelario of
Santa Fe.

Size: 196 cm. x 56 cm.
Count: 16 warps, 80 wefts.
Edge Finish: completely stitched over.

	Fiber	Type of Yarn	Spin	Twist	Ply	Color	Dye
Warp	Wool	Handspun	Z		1	White	Natural
Weft	Wool	Handspun	Z		1	White	Natural
	Wool	Handspun	Z		1	Orange	Aniline
	Wool	Handspun	Z		1	Olive	Aniline
	Wool	Handspun	Z		1	Light green	Aniline
	Wool	Handspun	Z		1	Lavender	Aniline

38

Blanket
55.20.49

Date: ca. 1900
Gift of Mrs. Richard Wetherill

Rio Grande, Chimayo.
Woven in one piece.

Size: 151 cm. x 67 cm.
Count: 13 warps, 30 wefts.
Edge Finish: completely stitched over.

	Fiber	Type of Yarn	Spin	Twist	Ply	Color	Dye
Warp	Wool	Handspun	Z	S	2	White	Natural
Weft	Wool	Handspun	Z		1	White	Natural
	Wool	Handspun	Z		1	Brown	Natural
	Wool	Handspun	Z		1	Orange	Aniline
	Wool	Handspun	Z		1	Pink	Aniline
	Wool	Handspun	Z		1	Lavender	Aniline
	Wool	Handspun	Z		1	Yellow	Aniline

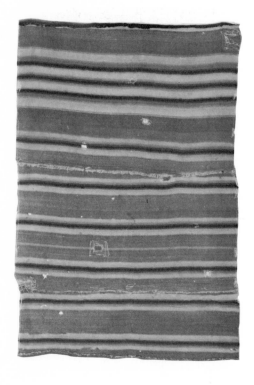

39

Fragment of a Serape
55.20.50

Date: ca. 1900
Gift of Mrs. Richard Wetherill

Made up of fragments pieced together.

Size: 99 cm. x 69 cm.
Count: 12 warps, 60 wefts.
Edge Finish: missing, completely stitched over with sewing
machine.

	Fiber	Type of Yarn	Spin	Twist	Ply	Color	Dye
Warp	Wool	Handspun	Z		1	White	Natural
Weft	Wool	Handspun	Z		1	White	Natural
	Wool	Handspun	Z		1	Orange	Aniline
	Wool	Handspun	Z		1	Black	Aniline
	Wool	Handspun	Z		1	Green	Aniline
	Wool	Handspun	Z		1	Pink	Aniline

40

Child's Poncho
63.34.165

Date: ca. 1910
Gift of Mr. and Mrs. Gilbert Maxwell

Rio Grande, Chimayo.
Woven in one piece with opening in center for head.

Size: 120.5 cm. x 57 cm.
Count: 22 warps, 70 wefts.
Edge Finish: warp, knotted chain; weft, last two warps are
paired.

	Fiber	Type of Yarn	Spin	Twist	Ply	Color	Dye
Warp	Cotton	String	Z	S	2	White	Natural
Weft	Wool	Handspun	Z		1	White	Natural
	Wool	Handspun	Z		1	Black	Aniline
	Wool	Handspun	Z		1	Red	Aniline
	Wool	Handspun	Z		1	Blue/Gray	Aniline

41

Rug
57.6.1

Date: 1900–30
Gift of Mrs. Willis S. Clayton, Jr.

Rio Grande, Chimayo.
Woven in one piece.

Size: 97.5 cm. x 46 cm.
Count: 10 warps, 30 wefts.
Edge Finish: warp, six warps tied together; weft, last two
warps paired.

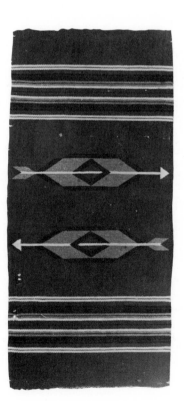

	Fiber	Type of Yarn	Spin	Twist	Ply	Color	Dye
Warp	Cotton	String				White	Natural
Weft	Wool	Commercial	Z	S	4	White	Aniline
	Wool	Commercial	Z	S	4	Black	Aniline
	Wool	Commercial	Z	S	4	Gray	Aniline
	Wool	Commercial	Z	S	4	Maroon	Aniline

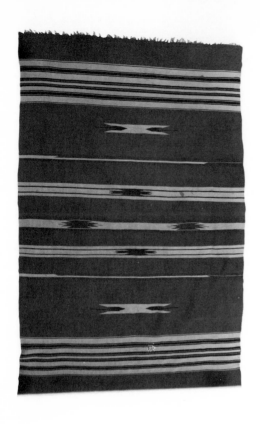

42

Blanket/Rug
57.6.2

Date: ca. 1920

Gift of Mrs. Willis S. Clayton, Jr.

Woven in one piece on a large loom.

Size: 196 cm. x 128 cm.

Count: 10 warps, 40 wefts.

Edge Finish: warp, five to seven warps tied together; weft, last warp paired.

	Fiber	Type of Yarn	Spin	Twist	Ply	Color	Dye
Warp	Cotton	String				White	Natural
Weft	Wool	Commercial	Z	S	4	White	Natural
	Wool	Commercial	Z	S	4	Rose	Aniline
	Wool	Commercial	Z	S	4	Gray	Aniline
	Wool	Commercial	Z	S	4	Black/Red	Aniline

43

Colcha, or embroidered bedcover
63.34.184

Date: ca. 1920

Gift of Mr. and Mrs. Gilbert Maxwell

Rio Grande.

Patched together from several pieces of cloth.

Twill weave with embroidery.

Size: 218 cm. x 176 cm.

Edge Finish: all hemmed under. A natural brown wool fringe is sewn on all four sides. Warp, weft, and embroidery all natural brown and white handspun wool.

44

Jerga
69.70.1

Date: nineteenth century
Gift of Mr. and Mrs. Bruce T. Ellis

Rio Grande.
Woven in two pieces and sewn down the center.
Twill weave.

Size: 183 cm. x 122 cm.
All natural brown and white handspun.

45

Jerga
69.70.3

Date: nineteenth century
Gift of Mr. and Mrs. Bruce T. Ellis

Rio Grande.
Pieced together from fragments of other jergas.
Diagonal twill.

Size: 189 cm. x 56 cm.
All natural white and brown handspun wool.

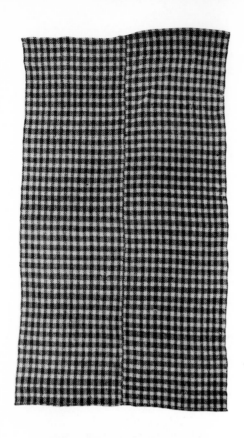

46

Jerga
63.34.75

Date: nineteenth century
Gift of Mr. and Mrs. Gilbert Maxwell

Rio Grande.
Woven in two pieces and sewn down the center.
Twill weave.

Size: 226 cm. x 128 cm.
All natural brown and white handspun wool.

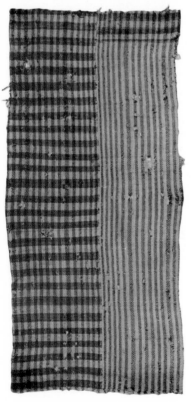

47

Jerga
69.70.4

Date: nineteenth century
Gift of Mr. and Mrs. Bruce T. Ellis

Woven in two pieces and sewn down the center.
Twill weave.

Size: 230 cm. x 116 cm.
All natural brown and white handspun wool.

48

Jerga
69.70.2

Date: nineteenth century
Gift of Mr. and Mrs. Bruce T. Ellis

Rio Grande.
Woven in two pieces and sewn down the center.
Diagonal twill weave.

Size: 408 cm. x 136 cm.
All natural brown and white handspun wool.

49

Jerga
69.70.5

Date: nineteenth century
Gift of Mr. and Mrs. Bruce T. Ellis

Rio Grande.
Woven in two pieces and sewn down the center.
Twill weave.

Size: 229.5 cm. x 128.5 cm.
All natural brown, white, and carded beige handspun.

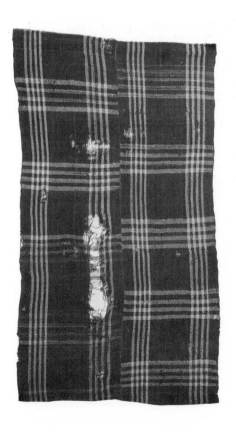

READING LIST

AMSDEN, C. A.
1934   *Navajo Weaving, Its Technic and Its History* (Glorieta, N.M.: Rio Grande Press, Inc.).
BENNETT, N. and T. BIGHORSE
1971   *Working with the Wool* (Flagstaff: Northland Press).
BOYD, E.
1974   *Popular Arts of Spanish New Mexico* (Santa Fe: Museum of New Mexico).
CERNY, C.
1975   *Navajo Pictorial Weaving* (Santa Fe: Museum of New Mexico Foundation).
DEDERA, D.
1975   *Navajo Rugs: How to Find, Evaluate, Buy and Care for Them* (Flagstaff: Northland Press).
DOUGLAS, F.
       Indian leaflet series, Leaflets of the Denver Art Museum, nos. 3, 21, 56, 59–60, 71, 89, 92–93, 94–95, 113, 116 (Denver: Denver Art Museum).
DUTTON, B.
1961   *Navajo Weaving Today* (Santa Fe: Museum of New Mexico Press).
HOLLISTER, U. S.
1903   *The Navajo and His Blanket* (Denver: United States Colortype Co.).
JAMES, G. W.
1920   *Indian Blankets and Their Makers* (Chicago: A. C. McClurg & Co.).
KAHLENBERG, M. H. and A. BERLANT
1972   *The Navajo Blanket* (New York: Praeger Publishers, Inc.).
KENT, K. P.
1957   *The Cultivation and Weaving of Cotton in the Prehistoric Southwestern United States*, Transactions of the American Philosophical Society, vol. 47, no. 2 (Philadelphia: American Philosophical Society).
1961   *Navajo Weaving* (Phoenix: The Heard Museum).
MC NITT, F.
1962   *The Indian Traders* (Norman: University of Oklahoma Press).
MATTHEWS, W.
1884   *Navajo Weavers*, Third Annual Report of the Bureau of American Ethnology, pp. 371–91 (Washington, D.C.: Government Printing Office).
MAXWELL, G.
1963   *Navajo Rugs—Past, Present and Future* (Palm Desert State: Desert-Southwest, Inc.).
MERA, H. P.
1948   *Navajo Textile Arts* (Santa Fe: Laboratory of Anthropology).
1949   *The Alfred I. Barton Collection of Southwestern Textiles* (Santa Fe: San Vicente Foundation).
MOORE, J. B.
1911   *The Navajo* (Denver: Williamson-Haffner Co.).
NEWCOMB, F. and G. REICHARD
1975   *Sandpaintings of the Navajo Shooting Chant* (New York: Dover Publications, Inc.).

PENDLETON, M.
1974   *Navajo and Hopi Weaving Techniques* (New York: Collier Books).
REICHARD, G. A.
1963   *Navajo Shepherd and Weaver* (New York: J. J. Augustin).
STOUT, C.
1974   *Saltillo and Rio Grande Weaving* (Albuquerque: Maxwell Museum of Anthropology).
UNDERHILL, R.
1944   *Pueblo Crafts* (Washington, D.C.: U.S. Department of the Interior).
WHEAT, J. B.
1975   *Patterns and Sources of Navajo Weaving* (Denver: The Printing Establishment).
WHEELWRIGHT, M. C.
1946   *Hail Chant and Water Chant* (Santa Fe: Museum of Navajo Ceremonial Art, Navajo Religion Series).
WYMAN, L. C., ED.
1957   *Beautyway: A Navajo Ceremonial* (Princeton, N.J.: Princeton University Press, Bollingen Series).
1970   *Blessingway* (Tucson: University of Arizona Press).